P9-BIQ-494

ALL ABOUT PARTICLES

A little book to make the
Japanese language manageable ...
and to say I'm so sorry for
not teaching you Japanese ☺

♡
mom

ALL ABOUT PARTICLES

Naoko Chino

Kodansha International
Tokyo • New York • London

Distributed in the United States by Kodansha America, Inc., 114 Fifth Avenue, New York, N.Y. 10011, and in the United Kingdom and continental Europe by Kodansha Europe Ltd., 95 Aldwych, London WC2B 4JF. Published by Kodansha International Ltd., 17-14 Otowa 1-chome, Bunkyo-ku, Tokyo 112, and Kodansha America, Inc.

Copyright © 1991 by Kodansha International Ltd.
All rights reserved. Printed in Japan.
First edition, 1991
95 96 97 98 99 10 9 8 7 6 5

Library of Congress Cataloging-in-Publication Data
Chino, Naoko.
    All about particles / Naoko Chino. – 1st ed.
      p. cm. – (Power Japanese series)
    ISBN 0-87011-954-0 (USA) :   – ISBN 4-7700-1501-1 (Japan) :
    1. Japanese language--Particles. I. Title. II. Series.
PL601.C49 1991   90-5001
495.6'82421–dc20   CIP

CONTENTS

Preface	7			
Wa は	10	Shika しか	72
Ga が	12	Nomi のみ	73
Mo も	23	Kiri きり	74
-Te mo (-de mo)		No de ので	75
ても (でも)	26	Mono de もので	76
De mo でも	27	Keredomo けれども	76
To と	29	Tokoro de ところで	78
To wa とは	34	No ni のに	79
Ya や	35	Kuse ni くせに	80
To ka とか	36	Mono no ものの	81
Nado など	37	Tokoro ga ところが	82
Ka か	39	-Ba ば	83
De で	42	-Tara たら	85
Ni に	45	Nara なら	87
E へ	52	Mono nara ものなら	88
Kara から	52	Tokoro ところ	89
Made まで	56	Mono o ものを	91
No の	58	-Nagara ながら	91
O を	61	-Tari たり	92
Kurai (gurai)		Shi し	94
くらい (ぐらい)	64	Tomo とも	95
Hodo ほど	65	Yara やら	97
Bakari ばかり	67	Dano だの	99
Dake だけ	69	Nari なり	100

-Te wa (-de wa)
  ては (では)   102
Dokoro どころ   104
Toshite として   104
Yori より   105
Sae さえ   108
Sura すら   109
Koso こそ   109

Sentence-ending Particles
Ne ね   110
Yo よ   112
Wa わ   113
Ka na かな   114
Kashira かしら   115
Na な   116
Sa さ   118
Koto こと   118
-Kke っけ   119
-Tteba ってば   120
I い   120
Mono もの   121
Ze ぜ   122
Zo ぞ   123
Mono ka ものか   124
Ni に   124

Index   125

Preface

Some things are easier to learn than others. Take, for instance, Japanese nouns, verbs, adjectives, and adverbs. Once you have a little grammar under your belt, you can pick them up and squirrel them away with relative ease. For some reason, though, this doesn't work with particles. They can't be looked up, pinned down, or pigeonholed in the same way that their fellows can. Yet their correct usage is essential to speaking Japanese with any degree of fluency.

Why are particles so elusive? Because particles are next to meaningless as isolated entities. A particle, in fact, might be defined as a non-conjugating part of speech, bearing an absolute minimum of independent meaning, which attaches itself to other parts of speech and thereby places them in context. Thus, a statement consisting of a single particle wouldn't convey much meaning. But the addition of another word would make a world of difference. A phrase like *Tōkyō ni* (to Tokyo), for instance, would communicate something, but not *ni* by itself. The rule of thumb might be: Japanese particles have virtually no meaning bereft of context.

In this book, I propose to clarify the functions of a considerable number of particles, to describe their various usages, and, most important, to exemplify each and every usage with sample sentences. Only in this way—through context—can the student truly come to grips with the Japanese particle.

Don't be surprised by certain of the particles taken up here. For example, there is *-ba*, as in *nomeba* (if [you] drink). You may think that *-ba* is not a particle at all, but an inflection of the verb *nomu*. Grammatically speaking, however, *-ba* is one of a species of particle that follows conjugated verbs (in this case, *nome-*). Since *-ba* and others of its tribe are not only true particles but exhibit a multiplicity of usage well worth your attention, I have chosen to include them.

An effort has been made to present the particles in order of frequency—the more common first; the less, later. An attempt has also been made to group particles by meaning. Neither the ordering nor the grouping, however, is entirely consistent, since the two systems are now and then at loggerheads. A further complication is that some of the more basic particles have usages belonging more properly to an intermediate or advanced level of study. (All usages at these two levels are marked with asterisks.)

Cross references are provided where similarities exist between different particles. This was not done without some misgivings, for while certain particles may be basically alike, they are usually not true equivalents in the sense that one can replace another without even a slight change in meaning or a certain oddness creeping in. In particular, there are numerous comparisons between *wa* and *ga* because of the frequent interplay between these two particularly pesky particles.

For those who wish to test their proficiency through exercises or who want more sample sentences, see my *Gaikoku-jin no tame no joshi* (外国人のための助詞) published in Tokyo by Musashino Shoin (武蔵野書院).

Finally, I thank Suzuki Shigeyoshi and Michael Brase, my editors at Kodansha International, for their help. My sincere thanks also go to Jay Thomas, who did most of the translation in the body of the book and offered many valuable suggestions. Without the cooperation of these three, this book would never have come into being.

ALL ABOUT PARTICLES

1 — | WA | は

Note: *Wa* has several usages, but its basic function is to set off a topic (e.g., of conversation) from the rest of the sentence, which talks about the topic. Technically, *wa* does not indicate case (subject, object, etc.). However, in practical terms, it often (but not always) comes after the subject of the sentence. See also *-te wa* (#47) and *to wa* (#17).

1. Indicates that information is being presented about something that is already known or that has been identified.

あそこに赤い本がありますね。あれは漢字の本です。

Asoko ni akai hon ga arimasu ne. Are wa kanji no hon desu.

Over there is a red book, right. It's a *kanji* book. / See the red book over there? That's a *kanji* book.

あの大学は、四谷駅の近くにあります。

Ano daigaku wa, Yotsuya-eki no chikaku ni arimasu.

That university—it's near Yotsuya Station. / That university is near Yotsuya Station.

2. Indicates a topic, which is then identified or explained.

明日は日曜日です。

Ashita wa nichiyōbi desu.

As for tomorrow, it's Sunday. / Tomorrow is Sunday.

鯨は魚ではありません。

Kujira wa sakana de wa arimasen.

As for the whale, it is not a fish. / The whale is not a fish.

Note: If *ga* replaces *wa* in these sentences, the noun which it follows is no longer being presented as a topic but as the subject of the predicate (see *ga*, #2, I-2). The switch from topic (*wa*) to definite subject (*ga*) lays stress on the latter. For example:

あさっては日曜日ですね。
違います。明日が日曜日ですよ。

Asatte wa nichiyōbi desu ne.
Chigaimasu. Ashita ga nichiyōbi desu yo.

The day after tomorrow is Sunday, isn't it.
You're wrong there. *Tomorrow* is Sunday.

3. In the construction N + *wa* N + *ga*, *wa* indicates a topic (the first noun) about which an aspect or quality (the second noun) is explained.

象は鼻が長いです。

Zō wa hana ga nagai desu.

The elephant—its nose is long. / Elephants have long noses.

竹本さんは性格が優しいです。

Takemoto-san wa seikaku ga yasashii desu.

As for Takemoto, her personality is gentle. / Takemoto has a gentle nature.

4. Used to show contrast between two items or ideas, both of which are signified by *wa*.

漢字は難しいですが、日本語の文法はあまり難しくな いんです。

Kanji wa muzukashii desu ga, Nihon-go no bunpō wa amari muzukashiku nai-n desu.

Kanji are difficult, but Japanese grammar is not very difficult.

北海道の冬は寒いですが、東京は暖かいです。

Hokkaidō no fuyu wa samui desu ga, Tōkyō wa atatakai desu.

The Hokkaido winter is cold, but [the] Tokyo [winter] is warm. / It's cold in Hokkaido in the winter, but warm in Tokyo.

Note: In some cases, only one item or idea is explicitly mentioned. For example, in the following sentence, the implication is that the person might go to a cheaper restaurant.

高いから、あのレストランには行きません。

Takai kara, ano resutoran ni wa ikimasen.
Because it's expensive, I won't go to that restaurant. / I am not going to *that* restaurant because it's too expensive.

Note: In its contrastive function, *wa* comes after other particles (e.g., *ni wa, de wa*). Two important exceptions are when it replaces *ga* and *o*, as in the next example.

バターを買いましたか。
マーガリンは買いましたが、バターは買いませんでした。

Batā o kaimashita ka.
Māgarin wa kaimashita ga, batā wa kaimasen deshita.

Did you buy some butter?
I bought some margarine, but I didn't buy any butter. / I bought some margarine, but not any butter.

5. In the forms V-*te wa iru* (first example below) and V-*masu* base followed by *wa* and *suru* (second and third examples), *wa* indicates emphasis. See also -*te wa* (#47).

コンピューターを持ってはいますが、まだ使って(は)いません。

Konpyūtā o motte wa imasu ga, mada tsukatte (wa) imasen.

I *own* a computer [I do own a computer], but I haven't used it yet.

あの人を知ってはいますが、あまり話したことはありません。

Ano hito o shitte wa imasu ga, amari hanashita koto wa arimasen.

I *know* him, but I haven't spoken to him much.

お茶は飲みましたが、時間がなかったので食事はしませんでした。

Ocha wa nomimashita ga, jikan ga nakatta no de shokuji wa shimasen deshita.

I had some tea, but since there wasn't much time, I didn't eat (have a meal).

2 — GA | が

I. Indicates the subject of the sentence or, with certain

verbs and adjectives, the object.

1. Indicates existence; used with such verbs as *aru*, *gozaimasu*, *iru*, *irassharu*.

あそこに私のボールペンがありますか。

Asoko ni watashi no bōrupen ga arimasu ka.

Is my ball-point pen over there?

あそこに郵便局があります。

Asoko ni yūbin-kyoku ga arimasu.

There's a post office over there.

私の会社には，女の人が50人以上います。

Watashi no kaisha ni wa, onna no hito ga gojū-nin ijō imasu.

There are more than fifty women in my company.

Note: *Wa* can replace *ga* in such sentences when (first example below) something is being contrasted (my ball-point pen, say, in contrast to my pencil) or when (second example) information is being presented about a subject already identified. See *wa* (#1, nos. 1, 4).

私のボールペンはあそこにありますか。

Watashi no bōrupen wa asoko ni arimasu ka.

Is my *ball-point pen* over there?

郵便局はどこにありますか。
（郵便局は）駅の前にあります。

Yūbin-kyoku wa doko ni arimasu ka.
(Yūbin-kyoku wa) eki no mae ni arimasu.

Where is the post office?
(The post office is) in front of the station.

2. Indicates the subject of the predicate.

あそこに桜が咲いています。

Asoko ni sakura ga saite imasu.

The cherry trees are blooming over there.

あの山を見て下さい。まだ雪が残っていますよ。

Ano yama o mite kudasai. Mada yuki ga nokotte imasu yo.

Look at that mountain. There's still snow on it. (Lit., . . . snow still remains.)

Note: When making a contrast, *wa* (#1, no. 4) can replace *ga*:

あそこに桜は咲いていますが、梅は咲いていません。

Asoko ni sakura wa saite imasu ga, ume wa saite imasen.

The cherry trees are blooming over there, but the plum trees are not.

3. Indicates the subject of an intransitive verb.

戸が開きました。

To ga akimashita.

The door opened.

雨が降っている。

Ame ga futte iru.

It's raining.

Note: *Wa* (#1, no. 4) can replace *ga* for contrastive purposes:

雨は降っているが、雪はまだ降っていません。

Ame wa futte iru ga, yuki wa mada futte imasen.

It's raining, but it's not snowing yet.

4. Indicates the subject of the sentence when new, as-yet-unknown information is being presented.

こちらが山田さんです。

Kochira ga Yamada-san desu.

This is Mr. Yamada. (a personal introduction)

昨日友達のジャックがあなたに会いたいと言っていました。

Kinō tomodachi no Jakku ga anata ni aitai to itte imashita.

Yesterday my friend Jack said that he wanted to meet you.

Note: Here again *wa* (#1, no. 4) can replace *ga* for contrastive purposes:

ご紹介します。こちらが山田さんで、こちらは鈴木さんです。

*Goshōkai shimasu. Kochira ga Yamada-san de, kochira **wa** Suzuki-san desu.*

Let me do the introductions. This is Mr. Yamada, and this is Ms. Suzuki.

5. Used with interrogative words in questions.

a) In general questions:

どの人が課長ですか。

*Dono hito **ga** kachō desu ka.*

Which one [person] is the section chief?

誰が一番早くきましたか。

*Dare **ga** ichiban hayaku kimashita ka.*

Who came [arrived] first?

Note: *Wa* (#1, nos. 1, 2) can replace *ga* if a topic is being presented:

課長はどの人ですか。

*Kachō **wa** dono hito desu ka.*

The section chief—which one [person] is he? / Which one is the section chief?

b) In asking for a choice:

すしとてんぷらとどちらが好きですか。

*Sushi to tenpura to dochira **ga** suki desu ka.*

Which do you like better, sushi or tempura?

中国語と日本語と、どちらがむずかしいですか。

*Chūgoku-go to Nihon-go to, dochira **ga** muzukashii desu ka.*

Which is more difficult, Chinese or Japanese?

6. Indicates the subject of a relative clause.

先週私が見た映画はつまらなかった。

*Senshū watashi **ga** mita eiga wa tsumaranakatta.*

The movie I saw last week was boring.

1週間で私が読む本は4冊です。

*Isshūkan de watashi **ga** yomu hon wa yonsatsu desu.*

I read four books a week [in one week]. (Lit., Four books

is what I read in one week.)

Note: *No* (#17, I-5) may replace *ga* in this usage.

7. Indicates the subject of a clause ending in *ka*.

なぜ彼がそんなことをやったか、わかりません。

Naze kare ga sonna koto o yatta ka, wakarimasen.

I don't know why he did that [lit., . . . something like that].

どうして彼女があんなつまらない本を読んでいるのか、不思議です。

Dō shite kanojo ga anna tsumaranai hon o yonde iru no ka, fushigi desu.

It is a mystery to me [beyond me] why she's reading such a boring book [a boring book like that].

8. Indicates the subject of a subordinate or conditional clause when it is different from the subject of the main clause.

a) Subordinate clauses.

母が日本にくる前に、（私は）この部屋をきれいに掃除しなければならない。

Haha ga Nihon ni kuru mae ni, [watashi wa] kono heya o kirei ni sōji shinakereba naranai.

Before my mother comes to Japan, I have to make this room nice and clean.

母が来たとき、私はごちそうを作った。

Haha ga kita toki, watashi wa gochisō o tsukutta.

When my mother came, I prepared quite a spread.

母が来たあと、私は買物に出かけた。

Haha ga kita ato, watashi wa kaimono ni dekaketa.

After my mother came, I went out shopping.

b) Conditional clauses.

あの人が行くんだったら、私は行かない。

Ano hito ga iku-n dattara, watashi wa ikanai.

If he's going, I am not.

あなたがそう言うなら、納豆を食べてみます。

Anata ga sō iu nara, nattō o tabete mimasu.

If you say so [if you recommend it, insist, etc.], I'll try some fermented beans.

9. Indicates the object of verbs of ability (*dekiru*, *wakaru*, and the potential forms of verbs).

阿部さんはゴルフができます。

Abe-san wa gorufu ga dekimasu.

Abe can play [lit., do] golf.

岡田さんはピアノが弾けます。

Okada-san wa piano ga hikemasu.

Okada can play the piano.

山田さんは中国語がわかります。

Yamada-san wa Chūgoku-go ga wakarimasu.

Yamada understands Chinese.

Note: *Wa* (#1, no. 4) can replace *ga* to create a contrast:

山田さんは、中国語はわかりますが、英語はわかりません。

Yamada-san wa, Chūgoku-go wa wakarimasu ga, Eigo wa wakarimasen.

Yamada understands Chinese, but not English.

10. Indicates the object of verbs of sensation (*mieru* and *kikoeru*) as well as *suru* in certain uses.

ここから富士山が見えます。

Koko kara Fuji-san ga miemasu.

Mt. Fuji can be seen from here. / You can see Mt. Fuji from here.

朝の台所は、コーヒーの香りがします。

Asa no daidokoro wa, kōhī no kaori ga shimasu.

The kitchen smells of coffee in the morning. / In the morning you can smell coffee [brewing] in the kitchen.

Note: *Wa* (#1, no. 4) can replace *ga* for contrast:

ここから富士山は見えますが、登る人の姿は見えません。

Koko kara Fuji-san wa miemasu ga, noboru hito no sugata wa miemasen.

You can see Mt. Fuji from here, but not the figures of the people climbing it.

11. Indicates the object of verbs and adjectives of necessity (*hitsuyō da, iru*).

私はお金が要る。

Watashi wa okane ga iru.
I need money.

交通の安全のため、厳しい規則が必要です。

Kōtsū no anzen no tame, kibishii kisoku ga hitsuyō desu.

Strict rules are needed for traffic safety.

Note: *Wa* (#1, no. 4) replaces *ga* when a contrast is being made:

私は、お金は要るが、物は要らない。

Watashi wa, okane wa iru ga, mono wa iranai.

I need money, but I don't need things.

12. Indicates the object of adjectives of desire (*hoshii* and the *-tai* form of verbs). Compare the use of *o* (#18, no. 5) with the *-garu* and *-tai* forms of verbs.

時間とお金が欲しい。

Jikan to okane ga hoshii.
I want time and money.

冷たいものが飲みたい。

Tsumetai mono ga nomitai.
I want something cold to drink.

Note: *Wa* (#1, no. 4) replaces *ga* when a contrast is being made:

冷たいものは飲みたいが、温かいものは要りません。

Tsumetai mono wa nomitai ga, atatakai mono wa irimasen.

I'd like to drink something cold, but not anything hot.

13. Indicates the object of verbs and adjectives of emo-

tion (*suki da, kirai da, ureshii, kanashii, kowai, shinpai suru*, etc.). Compare the use of *o* (#18, no. 5) with verbs in the *-tai* and *-garu* forms.

私はモーツァルトが大好きです。

Watashi wa Mōtsaruto ga daisuki desu.

I love Mozart.

ジョンさんは納豆が嫌いです。

Jon-san wa nattō ga kirai desu.

John doesn't like fermented soybeans.

秋になると台風が心配です。

Aki ni naru to taifū ga shinpai desu.

In the fall, typhoons are a worry [a problem].

花子はこんなすばらしいプレゼントをくれたんですよ。その気持ちが嬉しいです。

Hanako wa konna subarashii purezento o kureta-n desu yo. Sono kimochi ga ureshii desu.

Hanako gave me this wonderful present. I'm so pleased by her thoughtfulness.

Note: *Wa* (#1, no. 4) can be substituted for *ga* to create a contrast:

ジムさんは納豆は嫌いだが、するめは大好きです。

Jimu-san wa nattō wa kirai da ga, surume wa daisuki desu.

Jim doesn't like fermented soybeans, but he loves dried cuttlefish.

14. Indicates the object of adjectives of ability (*jōzu na, heta na, tokui na, kiyō na*, etc.).

新しい首相は、俳句が上手だそうです。

Atarashii shushō wa, haiku ga jōzu da sō desu.

The new prime minister is said to be good at haiku.

小川さんは語学が得意で、フランス語もイタリア語もできます。

Ogawa-san wa gogaku ga tokui de, Furansu-go mo Itaria-go mo dekimasu.

Ogawa is good at languages; she can speak both French and Italian.

Note: *Wa* (#1, no. 4) replaces *ga* when a contrast is intended:

新しい首相は、俳句は上手ですが、政治はまあまあです。

Atarashii shushō wa, haiku wa jōzu desu ga, seiji wa māmā desu.

The new prime minister is good at haiku, but his politics are just so-so.

II. Used between clauses (and sometimes at the end of sentences), usually with the meaning "but."

1. Used between two clauses to indicate that they are opposed in meaning (cf. II-3, below): "but, although."

この頃昼は暖かいんですが、夜は寒くなりました。

Konogoro hiru wa atatakai-n desu ga, yoru wa samuku narimashita.

Lately, the days are warm, but the nights have turned cold. / It's warm during the daytime these days, but cold at night.

私の家からスーパーは近いんですが、駅は遠いんです。

Watashi no ie kara sūpā wa chikai-n desu ga, eki wa tōi-n desu.

The supermarket is close to my house, but the train station is far away.

2. Indicates that a given subject has two different qualities: "but, although."

桜の花はきれいだが、香りがない。

Sakura no hana wa kirei da ga, kaori ga nai.

Cherry blossoms are pretty, but they have no fragrance.

この映画は面白いが、長すぎますね。

Kono eiga wa omoshiroi ga, nagasugimasu ne.

This movie is interesting, but it's just too long.

3. Connects two clauses without any adversative implication (cf. II-1, above): "and."

谷さんは頭がいいが、横田さんもいいです。

Tani-san wa atama ga ii ga, Yokota-san mo ii desu.

Tani is intelligent, and so is Yokota.

昨日富士山を初めて見ましたが，きれいでした。

Kinō Fuji-san o hajimete mimashita ga, kirei deshita.

I saw Mt. Fuji for the first time yesterday, and it was beautiful.

4. Indicates a preliminary remark.

Note: This type of sentence is often terminated after *ga*, at which point the interlocutor, sensing what it is to follow, takes up the thread of conversation.

私，広野と申しますが、ご主人はいらっしゃいますか。

Watashi, Hirono to mōshimasu ga, goshujin wa irasshaimasu ka.

My name is Hirono. Is your husband home?

先日お願いしたことですが、どうなりましたでしょうか。

Senjitsu onegai shita koto desu ga, dō narimashita deshō ka.

About the request I made several days ago, how has it turned out [has there been any progress]?

5. Used at the end of the sentence.

Note: These usages are essentially the same as those in II-4, above, except that the second clause isn't stated outright. (Words in brackets show only one of various imaginable contexts.)

a) Implies an unstated meaning that is in contrast to the one stated: "Well, yes, but."

おっしゃることはもっともですが……

Ossharu koto wa mottomo desu ga . . .

What you say is quite right, but . . . [it's difficult to implement now].

b) Softens a refusal: "I am sorry, but . . ."

部長は今会議中でございますが……

Buchō wa ima kaigi-chū de gozaimasu ga . . .

The division chief is in a meeting now . . . [so you'll have to wait to see him].

6. When used at the end of a sentence or clause and preceded by *to ii*, indicates that the speaker wants the event to come out as stated. Context determines whether or not the wish is actually realizable: "it would be nice if; it would have been nice if."

来年外国へ旅行できるといいが、だめのようです。

Rainen gaikoku e ryokō dekiru to ii ga, dame no yō desu.

It would be nice if I could make a trip abroad next year, but it seems as though I can't [seems impossible].

早く春が来るといいんだが……

Hayaku haru ga kuru to ii-n da ga . . .

It would be nice if spring came soon. / I hope spring comes soon.

彼女が独身だといいんだが……

Kanojo ga dokushin da to ii-n da ga . . .

I hope she is single. / (Or, knowing that she is not) I wish she were single.

7. Used idiomatically after contrastive verbs or adjectives: "whether or not."

a) After the *-ō* forms of contrastive verbs or adjectives.

私は助かろうが死のうがかまいません。

Watashi wa tasukarō ga shinō ga kamaimasen.

I don't care whether I live [lit., am saved] or die.

暑かろうが寒かろうが私は大丈夫です。

Atsukarō ga samukarō ga watashi wa daijōbu desu.

I'm all right [it doesn't bother me] whether it's hot or cold.

b) After the *-ō* and *-mai* forms of the same verb.

私が行こうが行くまいが、あなたには関係ないことで
す。

*Watashi ga ikō ga ikumai ga, anata ni wa kankei nai koto
desu.*

Whether I go or not has nothing to do with you [is not your
concern].

田中さんが信じようが信じまいが、ぼくははっきりと
ＵＦＯを見ました。

*Tanaka-san ga shinjiyō ga shinjimai ga, boku wa hakkiri to
yūfō o mimashita.*

Whether Tanaka believes it or not, I clearly saw a UFO.

8. Used in the expression V + *ga hayai ka*: "as soon as,
no sooner had."

窓を開けるが早いか、猫が飛び込んで来た。

Mado o akeru ga hayai ka, neko ga tobikonde kita.

No sooner had the window been opened than the cat jumped
in. / As soon as I opened the window the cat jumped in.

横になるが早いか、すぐ眠ってしまった。

Yoko ni naru ga hayai ka, sugu nemutte shimatta.

No sooner had I lain down than I fell asleep. / I fell asleep as
soon as my head hit the pillow.

3 — | MO | も

Note: See also *-te mo* (*-de mo*), #4, and *de mo*, #5.

1. Indicates that two words are equal in weight: "also,
too."

これは桜です。これも桜です。
Kore wa sakura desu. Kore mo sakura desu.
This is a cherry tree. This is a cherry tree, too.

ポールさんは日本語を勉強しています。ナンシーさん

も日本語を勉強しています。

Pōru-san wa Nihon-go o benkyō shite imasu. Nanshii-san mo Nihon-go o benkyō shite imasu.

Paul is studying Japanese. Nancy is also studying Japanese.

2. Showing similar nouns in parallel construction: "and, as well as, both."

私の会社には、アメリカ人も中国人もいます。

Watashi no kaisha ni wa, Amerika-jin mo Chūgoku-jin mo imasu.

There are both Americans and Chinese in my company.

花子さんは、すしもてんぷらも好きですよ。

Hanako-san wa, sushi mo tenpura mo suki desu yo.

Hanako likes both sushi and tempura.

3. Indicates an addition: "as well as, in addition."

これは黒ですが、白い靴もありますよ。

Kore wa kuro desu ga, shiroi kutsu mo arimasu yo.

These are black, but we have white shoes as well.

日本では子供だけでなく、大人もマンガを読んでいます。

Nihon de wa kodomo dake de naku, otona mo manga o yonde imasu.

In Japan, not only children read comic books, but adults as well.

4. Shows emphasis or absence of doubt concerning a question of time, quantity, etc.: "any number of times, continually."

あの映画は何度も見ました。

Ano eiga wa nando mo mimashita.

I have seen that movie any number of times.

このレストランは、いつも混んでいます。

Kono resutoran wa, itsu mo konde imasu.

This restaurant is always crowded.

5. Indicates total negation concerning a question of quality or quantity (accompanied by a negative verb): "no, nothing."

何もありませんが、召し上がって下さい。

Nani mo arimasen ga, meshiagatte kudasai.

We have nothing special to offer, but please help yourself. (Lit., There is nothing, but please eat [a conventional phrase].)

あの部屋には、だれもいませんよ。

Ano heya ni wa, dare mo imasen yo.

There is no one in that room.

6. To emphasize the extent of a number: "all of, as much (many) as."

スミスさんは、漢字を5000も知っています。

Sumisu-san wa, kanji o gosen mo shitte imasu.

Mr. Smith knows all of five thousand *kanji*.

そのアパートの家賃は、1ヶ月90万円もするそうです。

Sono apāto no yachin wa, ikkagetsu kyūjū-man-en mo suru sō desu.

The rent for that apartment is said to be as high as ¥900,000.

7. Indicates approximation (by showing an approximate upper limit) regarding number or quantity: "around, up to."

1時間もあれば、ホテルから空港へ行けます。

Ichi-jikan mo areba, hoteru kara kūkō e ikemasu.

If you have as much as an hour, you can get from the hotel to the airport. / You can get from the hotel to the airport inside an hour [in an hour or so].

5万円も出せば、いいカメラが買えますよ。

Go-man-en mo daseba, ii kamera ga kaemasu yo.

If you spend up to ¥50,000, you can get a good camera. / You can buy a good camera for ¥50,000.

4 — -TE MO (-DE MO)
ても（でも）

Note: Here we are concerned with *mo* in combination with the *-te (-de)* form of verbs and the *-kute* form of adjectives. See also *mo* (#3) and *de mo* (#5).

1. "Even if, even though."

明日天気が悪くても、ドライブに行きましょう。

Ashita tenki ga warukute mo, doraibu ni ikimashō.

Even if the weather is bad tomorrow, let's go for a drive. / Let's go for a drive tomorrow even if the weather's bad.

友達が作ってくれたので、あまりおいしくなくても料理は全部食べましたよ。

Tomodachi ga tsukutte kureta no de, amari oishiku nakute mo ryōri wa zenbu tabemashita yo.

Since a friend prepared the food [for me], I ate everything, even though it didn't taste very good.

2. After verbs, used in conjunction with interrogatives for emphasis: "no matter where (who, what, etc.)."

武田さんは、いくら飲んでも酔わないんですよ。

Takeda-san wa, ikura nonde mo yowanai-n desu yo.

No matter how much Takeda drinks, he doesn't get drunk.

お花見のときは、どこへ行っても人でいっぱいだ。

Ohanami no toki wa, doko e itte mo hito de ippai da.

During flower-viewing time, there are crowds of people wherever you go.

3. Emphasizes an approximate limit: "at the most."

そのカメラなら、高くても5万円くらいでしょう。

Sono kamera nara, takakute mo go-man-en kurai deshō.

At the most, that camera will cost around ¥50,000. (Lit., That camera, even if it's expensive, will be about ¥50,000.)

あの芝居は長くても3時間で終わりますよ。

Ano shibai wa nagakute mo san-jikan de owarimasu yo.

That play will last three hours at the most.

5 — | DE MO | でも |

Note: In all usages except no. 6, *de mo* can be replaced by the more informal *datte* (not included in this book). See also *mo*, #3, and *-te mo* (*-de mo*), #4.

1. Used after nouns to emphasize a hypothetical: "even, even if."

つまらない会議でも仕事ですから出なければなりません。

Tsumaranai kaigi de mo shigoto desu kara denakereba narimasen.

Even if it's a boring meeting, you have to attend since it's [part of] the job. / You have to attend even the boring meetings since it's [part of] the job.

嫌いな食べ物でも、体によければ食べた方がいいですね。

Kirai na tabemono de mo, karada ni yokereba tabeta hō ga ii desu ne.

Even if it's food you dislike, you should eat it if it's good for your health. / You should eat even food you dislike if it's good for your health.

2. Used after nouns for emphasis: "even."

その仕事は私でもできましたから、あなたならすぐできますよ。

Sono shigoto wa watashi de mo dekimashita kara, anata nara sugu dekimasu yo.

Since even I was able to do that work, you will be able to do it immediately. / If *I* can do it, you should be able to do it [handle that job] with ease.

動物でも人間の心がわかります。

Dōbutsu de mo ningen no kokoro ga wakarimasu.

Even animals can understand the human heart.

3. Used after an interrogative word for positive emphasis: "any- (one, where, etc.)."

ジョンさんは、日本料理なら何でも食べます。

Jon-san wa, Nihon-ryōri nara nan de mo tabemasu.

John will eat any [kind of] Japanese food.

私は、夜だったらいつでもいいですよ。

Watashi wa, yoru dattara itsu de mo ii desu yo.

As long as it's at night, any time is all right for me. / Any time at night is fine with me.

4. Used in the form *donna . . . de mo*: "whatever."

ヨーロッパへ行ったら、どんな美術館でも見てみたい。

Yōroppa e ittara, donna bijutsu-kan de mo mite mitai.

If I go to Europe, I'll want to see whatever museums [I can].

英語のできる人なら、どんな人でもかまいません。

Eigo no dekiru hito nara, donna hito de mo kamaimasen.

As long as it's someone who can speak English, it doesn't matter who it is. / Anyone who can speak English will do.

5. Used with two or more nouns which serve as examples of a larger list: "either . . . or (and others of a similar nature)."

松本さんは運動神経がいいので、テニスでも、ゴルフでもできますよ。

Matsumoto-san wa undō-shinkei ga ii no de, tenisu de mo, gorufu de mo dekimasu yo.

Given Matsumoto's good reflexes, he can play either tennis or golf [or any other sport].

片岡さんは、外国語に興味を持っているから、フランス語でも中国語でも、すぐ覚えてしまう。

Kataoka-san wa gaikoku-go ni kyōmi o motte iru kara, Furan-

su-go de mo Chūgoku-go de mo, sugu oboete shimau.

Since Kataoka is interested in foreign languages, he can easily pick up either French or Chinese [or any other language].

6. Indicates one possibility: ". . . or something."

映画でも見に行きませんか。

Eiga de mo mi ni ikimasen ka.

How about going to see a movie or something?

レコードでも聞きましょうか。

Rekōdo de mo kikimashō ka.

Shall we listen to a record or something?

6 — TO | と

I. Follows nouns; indicates such meanings as "and" and "with," and sets off names.

1. Joins nouns, usually two or three (but not phrases and clauses): "and."

Note: Contrast with *ya* (#8, no. 1).

アランさんとポールさんはフランス人です。

Aran-san to Pōru-san wa Furansu-jin desu.

Alain and Paul are French.

白いゆりと赤いばらの花を買いましょう。

Shiroi yuri to akai bara no hana o kaimashō.

Let's buy some white lilies and red roses.

2. Indicates a comparison or contrast: "and" or (when a choice is asked for) "or."

Note: In this usage, *to* must follow each of the nouns.

この会社とその会社とでは、資本金が違います。

Kono kaisha to sono kaisha to de wa, shihon-kin ga chi-gaimasu.

This company and that company have different amounts of capital.

りんごとみかんとどちらが好きですか。

Ringo to mikan to dochira ga suki desu ka.

Which do you like better, apples or mandarin oranges?

3. "Together, with."

社長は部長と食事をしています。

Shachō wa buchō to shokuji o shite imasu.

The company president is eating out with the division manager.

明日この問題について、先生と話すつもりです。

Ashita kono mondai ni tsuite, sensei to hanasu tsumori desu.

Tomorrow I intend to discuss this problem with my teacher [instructor, doctor, lawyer, etc.].

*4. Indicates a change or result (commonly used in the phrase *to naru*).

Note: *Ni* (#13, no. 8) is also used in this pattern; *to* is more formal and is commonly used in writing.

オリンピックの開会式の日となった。

Orinpikku no kaikai-shiki no hi to natta.

The day of the opening ceremony of the Olympics arrived. (Lit., It became the day of the opening ceremony of the Olympics.)

今年の海外旅行者は、1000万人となった。

Kotoshi no kaigai-ryokōsha wa, issen-man-nin to natta.

[The number of] overseas travelers this year reached ten million.

*5. Following an expression of quantity, reinforces the negative idea of the sentence: "(not) as much as."

あの山に登るには、2時間とかかりません。

Ano yama ni noboru ni wa, ni-jikan to kakarimasen.

It won't take as long as [won't take even] two hours to climb that mountain.

あの会社とは2度と取引きをしたくない。

Ano kaisha to wa nido to torihiki o shitaku nai.

I don't want to have dealings with that company ever again. (Lit., I don't want to have dealings with that company two times [because I've dealt with them once already and know what they're like].)

II. Used after onomatopoeic adverbs, or follows a word, clause, or sentence and precedes such verbs as *iu*, *kiku*, and *omou* to indicate what someone said, asked, thought, etc.

1. Indicates what someone said, ordered, asked, etc.

山本さんが、あとで電話すると おっしゃいました。

Yamamoto-san ga, ato de denwa suru to osshaimashita.

Yamamoto said that she would phone later.

母が先生によろしくと 申しておりました。

Haha ga sensei ni yoroshiku to mōshite orimashita.

Mother said to give her regards to you (who are my teacher, doctor, etc.).

渡辺さんが9時までに事務所に来るように、と言っていました。

Watanabe-san ga kuji made ni jimu-sho ni kuru yō ni, to itte imashita.

Watanabe said that you should come to his office by nine o'clock. / Watanabe asked that you come to the office by nine o'clock.

2. Indicates what someone thinks or feels.

来年は、アメリカへ行こうと 考えています。

Rainen wa, Amerika e ikō to kangaete imasu.

I'm thinking of going to the United States next year.

電車は9時に出ると思いましたが、10時でした。

Densha wa kuji ni deru to omoimashita ga, jūji deshita.

I thought the train would leave at nine o'clock, but [it left at] ten. / Or, I thought the train was going to leave [was scheduled to leave] at nine o'clock, but it turned out to be ten.

3. Indicates the name of something, about which an explanation follows; usually used when the name alone would not be understood. Always used in the form *to iu* (or some variation): "that (who, which) is called, known as."

「世界」という雑誌を知っていますか。

"Sekai" to iu zasshi o shitte imasu ka.

Do you know the magazine *Sekai*?

ブルー・スカイズというホテルに泊まりました。

Burū Sukaizu to iu hoteru ni tomarimashita.

I stayed at a hotel called Blue Skies.

まず、田中という部長に書類をもらって下さい。

Mazu, Tanaka to iu buchō ni shorui o moratte kudasai.

First of all, get the documents from a section manager named Tanaka.

4. Used after onomatopoeic adverbs.

小川がさらさらと、道のそばを流れていた。

Ogawa ga sarasara to, michi no soba o nagarete ita.

A sparkling brook flowed alongside the road.

星がきらきらと輝いています。

Hoshi ga kirakira to kagayaite imasu.

The stars are twinkling.

III. Follows verbs and adjectives to form a conditional: "if, unless, whether or not."

1. Indicates that a second action follows immediately upon the action preceding it; often used with *sugu* (immediately, right away): "as soon as."

Note: *Nari* (#46, no. 3) and *-tara* (#35, no. 5) can be used here with much the same meaning.

朝起きるとすぐ、カーテンを開けます。

Asa okiru to sugu, kāten o akemasu.

As soon as I get up in the morning, I open the curtains.

昨日は会社の仕事が終わると、まっすぐ家に帰った。

Kinō wa kaisha no shigoto ga owaru to, massugu ie ni kaetta.

Yesterday, as soon as work was over, I went home. / I went straight home after work yesterday.

2. Indicates the inevitability of a second action following the one preceding it: "when, as."

日本では春になると桜が咲きます。

Nihon de wa haru ni naru to sakura ga sakimasu.

When spring comes in Japan, the cherry trees bloom. / In Japan, the cherry trees bloom with the coming of spring.

車が多くなると交通事故が増えます。

Kuruma ga ōku naru to kōtsū-jiko ga fuemasu.

As (the number of) cars increases, the (incidence of) traffic accidents rises. / The more cars there are, the more traffic accidents occur.

不景気になると失業者が増えます。

Fu-keiki ni naru to shitsugyō-sha ga fuemasu.

When there is a recession, the number of jobless increases.

3. Indicates a hypothetical condition: "if, unless."

Note: *-Ba* (#34, no. 1) and *-tara* (#35, no. 1) have much the same meaning. Compare also *-ba* (#34, no. 2).

山田さんが来ないと会議が始められません。

Yamada-san ga konai to kaigi ga hajimeraremasen.

If Yamada doesn't come, the meeting can't be started. / We can't start the meeting unless Yamada comes.

明日、天気がいいと野球ができます。

Ashita, tenki ga ii to yakyū ga dekimasu.

If the weather is good tomorrow, we can play baseball.

4. Indicates that something has been learned as a result of a certain action: "when, after, as a result of."

Note: -*Tara* (#35, no. 4) can also be used with this meaning.

銀行へ行くと、もう閉まっていた。

Ginkō e iku to, mō shimatte ita.

When I went to the bank, [I found] it was already closed.

交番で道をきくと、その会社はすぐ見つかった。

Kōban de michi o kiku to, sono kaisha wa sugu mitsukatta.

After asking the way at a police box, I found [located] the company right away.

5. Used with two verbs (either two different verbs ending in -*yō*/-*ō*, or the same verb repeated, the first ending in -*yō*/-*ō*, the second in the negative -*mai*); indicates a lack of concern over which of the two events occurs: "whether . . . or (not)."

"円"が強くなろうと弱くなろうと、私の生活には関係ありません。

"En" ga tsuyoku narō to yowaku narō to, watashi no seikatsu ni wa kankei arimasen.

Whether the yen gets stronger or grows weaker [rises or falls], it has no effect on my [daily] life.

彼女が一人でパーティーに行こうと行くまいと、私はかまいません。

Kanojo ga hitori de pātī ni ikō to iku mai to, watashi wa kamaimasen.

I don't care whether she goes to the party alone or not.

7 — | TO WA | とは

1. Indicates a word or phrase being defined, or for which a definition is being asked.

UNとは、国連のことです。

UN to wa, kokuren no koto desu.

"UN" refers to the United Nations.

リーダーの条件**とは**何でしょうか。

*Rīdā no jōken **to wa** nan deshō ka.*

What are the prerequisites of leadership?

*2. Used between two clauses that are opposed in meaning: the first clause represents a concession to the second (usually in the form *to wa ie*): "though, even though."

政府を信用していない**とはいえ**、政府のやり方に従わないわけにはいかない。

*Seifu o shin'yō shite inai **to wa ie**, seifu no yarikata ni shitagawanai wake ni wa ikanai.*

Even though you don't trust the government, you [still] have to adhere to its way of doing things. / You may not trust the government, but you must still adhere to its ways of doing things.

春**とはいえ**まだ寒い。

*Haru **to wa ie** mada samui.*

Even though it's spring, it's still cold.

8 — | YA | や |

1. Joins nouns to indicate a non-exhaustive list of items: "such things as, and . . . and."

Note: *Ya* implies that the items stated are taken as examples from a larger group of items. In contrast, *to* (#6, I-1) implies that the items stated are the only ones under consideration. *Ya* is often combined with *nado* ("and such"), reinforcing its basic meaning.

テーブルの上に、おすし**や**やきとり**や**てんぷらなどがあります。

*Tēburu no ue ni, osushi **ya** yakitori **ya** tenpura nado ga arimasu.*

On the table, there are such things as sushi, *yakitori*, and tempura.

私の部屋には、コンピューターやステレオが置いてあります。

Watashi no heya ni wa, konpyūtā ya sutereo ga oite arimasu.

In my room there is a computer, a stereo, and such.

*2. In the idiomatic expression *ya ina ya* (following a verb root): "as soon as, no sooner had."

駅に着くやいなや、電車が出てしまった。

Eki ni tsuku ya ina ya, densha ga dete shimatta.

No sooner had I arrived at the station than the train left.

おふろに入るやいなや、電話が鳴った。

Ofuro ni hairu ya ina ya, denwa ga natta.

No sooner had I gotten into the bath than the phone rang.

9 — | TO KA | とか

1. Joins nouns, verbs (clauses), or adjectives to indicate several representative items from a much larger possible listing: "among other things, such things as."

Note: When used with nouns, *to ka* has the same meaning as *ya* (#8, no. 1), but is more informal. See also *ka* (#11, II-4).

昨日デパートで、セーターとかくつとかを買った。

Kinō depāto de, sētā to ka kutsu to ka o katta.

Yesterday I bought a sweater, shoes, and some other things at the department store.

休みにはジョギングをするとか、テニスをするとかしています。

Yasumi ni wa jogingu o suru to ka, tenisu o suru to ka shite imasu.

When I'm off work, I do things like jogging and playing tennis.

*2. Used after pairs of words of opposite meaning, indicating uncertainty.

川口さんは、あの銀行に勤めるとか勤めないとか言っていましたが、どうなりましたか。

*Kawaguchi-san wa, ano ginkō ni tsutomeru **to ka** tsutomenai **to ka** itte imashita ga, dō narimashita ka.*

Kawaguchi was saying that he'd work for that bank and then that he wouldn't. Whatever happened?

あの人はそのときによって、仕事が面白いとか面白くないとか言うので、どちらなのかわかりません。

*Ano hito wa sono toki ni yotte, shigoto ga omoshiroi **to ka** omoshiroku nai **to ka** iu no de, dochira na no ka wakarimasen.*

Depending on which day it is, she says she likes her work or she doesn't like it, so I don't know whether she does or not.

10 — NADO | など

Note: *Nanka* is an informal equivalent, and *nazo* and *nanzo* more formal equivalents.

1. Indicates that a series of items is non-exhaustive; often used with *ya* (#8, no. 1): "etc., and so forth."

そのへんにはレストランやディスコや映画館などがあります。

*Sono hen ni wa resutoran ya disuko ya eiga-kan **nado** ga arimasu.*

There are restaurants, discos, movie theaters, and so forth around there [in that area].

私は、みかんやりんごやバナナなど、くだものなら何でも好きです。

*Watashi wa, mikan ya ringo ya banana **nado**, kudamono nara nan de mo suki desu.*

I like any kind of fruit: mandarin oranges, apples, bananas.

2. Indicates a tentative suggestion: "or something (somewhere, etc.)."

来週の旅行は箱根**など**どうですか。

*Raishū no ryokō wa Hakone **nado** dō desu ka.*

How about some place like Hakone for next week's trip? / How would Hakone be for the trip next week?

プレゼントを買うなら、真珠のブローチ**なんか**いいんじゃないんですか。

*Purezento o kau nara, shinju no burōchi **nanka** ii-n ja nai-n desu ka.*

If you're going to buy a present, wouldn't something like a pearl brooch be all right? / If you're going to buy a present, a pearl brooch, or something like that, might be nice.

*3. Expresses humbleness: "such as, the likes of."

私**など**、そんなむずかしい試験にはとても合格できません。

*Watashi **nado**, sonna muzukashii shiken ni wa totemo gōkaku dekimasen.*

Someone like me could never pass a difficult examination like that. / There's no way that *I* [the likes of me] could pass such a difficult test.

橋本先生のご兄弟と違って、私の兄弟**なぞ**は、頭が悪い者ばかりです。

*Hashimoto-sensei no gokyōdai to chigatte, watashi no kyōdai **nazo** wa, atama ga warui mono bakari desu.*

Unlike Professor Hashimoto's [brother and sisters], none of my brothers and sisters, such as they are, is very bright.

*4. Used to emphasize the negative aspect of the situation, especially in a belittling manner: "anyone like, the likes of."

田中さん**など**は、とても社長にはなれない。

*Tanaka-san **nado** wa, totemo shachō ni wa narenai.*

There's no way that anyone like Tanaka [that the likes of Tanaka] could become president of the company.

あの人なんか、選挙に出てもだめですよ。

*Ano hito **nanka**, senkyo ni dete mo dame desu yo.*

It's no use for someone like him to run for election.

*5. Emphasizes the impossibility of the situation: "such, anything like."

そんな高いものなぞ、いただくわけにはいきません。

*Sonna takai mono **nazo**, itadaku wake ni wa ikimasen.*

I could never accept such an expensive thing (gift).

家なんか、とても買えない。

*Ie **nanka**, totemo kaenai.*

I could never buy anything like a house.

6. After verbs and adjectives: "something to the effect that."

山本さんがそのコンサートがとてもよかったなどと言っていましたよ。

*Yamamoto-san ga sono konsāto ga totemo yokatta **nado** to itte imashita yo.*

Yamamoto was saying that the concert was quite good [and such things]. / Yamamoto was saying something about the concert being very good.

彼はその仕事を自分がやったなどと言っている。

*Kare wa sono shigoto o jibun ga yatta **nado** to itte iru.*

He's saying such things as it was he that did that work. / He's saying that he was the one who did that job.

11 — | KA | か

I. Indicates a question; found at the end of a sentence.

1. Indicates a simple question.

これはだれの傘ですか。

*Kore wa dare no kasa desu **ka**.*

Whose umbrella is this?

明日のパーティーに行きますか。

Ashita no pātī ni ikimasu ka.

Are you going to the party tomorrow?

2. Indicates an inquiry about someone's feelings or intentions or a suggestion about something: "how about."

映画を見に行きませんか。

Eiga o mi ni ikimasen ka.

How about going to see a movie?

佐藤さんに聞いてみたらどうですか。

Satō-san ni kiite mitara dō desu ka.

How about asking Satō?

3. Indicates a rhetorical question.

こんなにきれいな所が、ほかにあるだろうか。

Konna ni kirei na tokoro ga, hoka ni aru darō ka.

Is there another place as lovely this? / Where else could you find a place as lovely as this?

そんな悪い人がいるものですか。

Sonna warui hito ga iru mono desu ka.

Are there people around as bad [awful] as that?

4. Indicates anger or censure: "So you . . .?"

また今日も、遅れて来たんですか。

Mata kyō mo, okurete kita-n desu ka.

So you're late again today?

まだこの仕事をしていないんですか。

Mada kono shigoto o shite inai-n desu ka.

You haven't done [finished] this work yet?

*5. Indicates that someone is talking to him- or herself.

今日は月曜日か。

Kyō wa getsuyōbi ka.

Today's Monday, is it?

そろそろ夏も終わりか。

Sorosoro natsu mo owari ka.

So summer's almost over, huh? / Well, it looks like summer's almost over.

II. Indicates a choice, doubt, uncertainty; found within a sentence.

1. Indicates a choice: "or, whether or not."

コーヒーか紅茶か飲みたいですね。

Kōhī ka kōcha ka nomitai desu ne.

I'd sure like to drink some coffee or tea. / Some coffee or tea would be nice, wouldn't it.

旅行に行くか行かないか、まだ決めていません。

Ryokō ni iku ka ikanai ka, mada kimete imasen.

I still haven't decided whether I'm going to take a trip or not.

広田さんはお酒が飲めるかどうか聞いてみましょう。

Hirota-san wa osake ga nomeru ka dō ka kiite mimashō.

Let's ask Hirota whether he drinks [alcoholic beverages] or not.

2. Indicates uncertainty about a state or reason: "I wonder."

かぜをひいたのか、頭が痛いんです。

Kaze o hiita no ka, atama ga itai-n desu.

I wonder if I've caught a cold—my head hurts. / I've got a headache. Maybe I've caught a cold.

試験があるのか、みんな図書館で勉強していますよ。

Shiken ga aru no ka, minna tosho-kan de benkyō shite imasu yo.

I wonder if there's a test—everyone's studying at the library.

3. Used with an interrogative word, indicating such meanings as "something, anything; someone, anyone."

だれか山田さんの電話番号を知っていますか。

Dare ka Yamada-san no denwa-bangō o shitte imasu ka.

Does anyone know Yamada's telephone number?

何か冷たいものが飲みたい。

Nani ka tsumetai mono ga nomitai.

I want to drink something cold. / I'd like something cold to drink.

4. Following other particles, indicates uncertainty or doubt. See also *to ka* (#9).

山田さんとかいう人から電話がありました。

Yamada-san to ka iu hito kara denwa ga arimashita.

There was a call from someone called Yamada or something or other.

彼女は、デパートでかブティックでか、どちらかで買物をしたいと言っていました。

Kanojo wa, depāto de ka butikku de ka, dochira ka de kaimono o shitai to itte imashita.

She said she wanted to do some shopping, at a department store or a boutique I think it was.

5. In the idiomatic expression *ka . . . -nai uchi ni*: "hardly had, no sooner had."

駅に着くか着かないうちに電車が来た。

Eki ni tsuku ka tsukanai uchi ni densha ga kita.

I had hardly arrived at the station when the train came.

おふろに入るか入らないうちに電話が鳴った。

Ofuro ni hairu ka hairanai uchi ni denwa ga natta.

No sooner had I gotten into the bath than the phone rang.

12 — DE | で

1. Indicates the location of an action: "at, in."

Note: Contrast with *ni* (#13, no. 2).

昨日銀座のレストランで晩ごはんを食べました。

Kinō Ginza no resutoran de bangohan o tabemashita.

Yesterday I had dinner at a restaurant in Ginza.

私の友達は、図書館で本を読んでいます。

Watashi no tomodachi wa, tosho-kan de hon o yonde imasu.

My friend [a friend of mine] is reading a book in the library.

2. Indicates a means or implement: "by, with."

私は日本へ船で来ました。

Watashi wa Nihon e fune de kimashita.

I came to Japan by boat.

ボールペンで書いて下さい。

Bōrupen de kaite kudasai.

Please write with a ball-point pen.

3. Indicates materials used: "of, from, with."

このケーキは、卵と砂糖で作ります。

Kono kēki wa, tamago to satō de tsukurimasu.

This cake is made of eggs and sugar.

昔、日本人は木と紙で作った家に住んでいました。

Mukashi, Nihon-jin wa ki to kami de tsukutta ie ni sunde imashita.

Long ago, the Japanese lived in houses made of wood and paper.

Note: *Kara* may replace *de* in this usage except when the raw material is unmistakably evident (as with paper, wood, glass, cloth, string, and leather), in which case *de* must be used. Compare *kara* (#15, I-6).

4. Indicates the greatest (largest, smallest, least, oldest, newest, etc.) within a given category: "in."

世界で一番高い山は何ですか。

Sekai de ichiban takai yama wa nan desu ka.

What is the highest mountain in the world?

これはこの村で一番古いお寺です。

Kore wa kono mura de ichiban furui otera desu.

This is the oldest temple in the village.

5. Indicates amount and scope: "within the space (time) of, in, for."

この本は1時間で読めますよ。

Kono hon wa ichi-jikan de yomemasu yo.

You can read this book in an hour.

あのテレビは10万円で買える。

Ano terebi wa jū-man-en de kaeru.

You can buy that TV set for ¥100,000.

6. Indicates the mode or condition of the agent of an action (not to be confused with the subject).

山田さんはアパートに1人で住んでいます。

Yamada-san wa apāto ni hitori de sunde imasu.

Yamada lives in an apartment by himself.

家族中でハワイへ旅行した。

Kazoku-jū de Hawai e ryokō shita.

I made a trip to Hawaii with the whole family.

7. Indicates time or age: "when, at the age of."

Note: Compare *ni* (#13, no. 3).

あの詩人は25歳で死んだ。

Ano shijin wa nijūgo-sai de shinda.

That poet died at the age of twenty-five.

戦争が終わって来年で50年になる。

Sensō ga owatte rainen de gojū-nen ni naru.

Next year will be the fiftieth year since the war ended.

8. Indicates the reason for something: "because of."

病気で旅行に行けなかった。

Byōki de ryokō ni ikenakatta.

Because I was sick, I couldn't go on the trip.

台風で電車が止まった。

Taifū de densha ga tomatta.

The train stopped on account of the typhoon.

13 — NI | に

1. Indicates where a person or thing is: "in, at, on."

a) Indicates a concrete place.

山田先生は、今図書館にいらっしゃいます。

Yamada-sensei wa, ima tosho-kan ni irasshaimasu.

Professor Yamada is in the library now.

電話帳は机の上にあります。

Denwa-chō wa tsukue no ue ni arimasu.

The phone book is on the desk.

b) Indicates an abstract place.

課長は今会議に出席しています。

Kachō wa ima kaigi ni shusseki shite imasu.

The section chief is now in conference.

彼は今でも演劇界に君臨しています。

Kare wa ima de mo engeki-kai ni kunrin shite imasu.

Even now he rules over [dominates] the theatrical world.

2. Indicates the location of an action: "in, at."

Note: In contrast to this use of *ni*, *de* (#12, no. 1) is used to indicate a one-time or short-term action.

a) Used with certain "non-action" verbs, which imply that the subject is permanently located in the place of action.

山田さんは現在四谷に住んでいます。

Yamada-san wa genzai Yotsuya ni sunde imasu.

Yamada lives in Yotsuya at present.

寺田さんは新宿の銀行に勤めています。

*Terada-san wa Shinjuku no ginkō **ni** tsutomete imasu.*

Terada works (is working) at a bank in Shinjuku.

Note: The verbs *hataraku* and *shigoto o suru* (to work) are preceded by *de*.

b) Used with verbs that indicate that an action has taken (or is to take) place and the resulting condition is (or will be) static. The last sentence exemplifies the parenthetical definition.

あのいすに座って本を読んでいる人は、誰ですか。

*Ano isu **ni** suwatte hon o yonde iru hito wa, dare desu ka.*

Who is the person sitting in that chair and reading a book?

山の上に雪が積もっていますね。

*Yama no ue **ni** yuki ga tsumotte imasu ne.*

Snow is piled up on top of the mountain, isn't it. / There is snow on the mountaintop, isn't there.

すみませんが、壁に掛かっている私のコートを取って
くれますか。

*Sumimasen ga, kabe **ni** kakatte iru watashi no kōto o totte kuremasu ka.*

Excuse me, but would you get my coat hanging on the wall?

新聞は机の上に置いて下さい。

*Shinbun wa tsukue no ue **ni** oite kudasai.*

Please put the newspaper on the desk.

3. Indicates time: "at, on, in; every, per."

a) Indicates the specific time at which something takes place.

会社は9時に始まります。

*Kaisha wa kuji **ni** hajimarimasu.*

Work [the office] begins at nine o'clock.

月曜日に大阪へ行きます。

*Getsuyōbi **ni** Ōsaka e ikimasu.*

I'm going to Osaka on Monday.

b) Indicates the interval of time during which something takes place.

１週間に１度テニスをします。

Isshūkan ni ichido tenisu o shimasu.

I play tennis once a week.

このバスは30分おきに来ます。

Kono basu wa sanjippun oki ni kimasu.

This bus comes every thirty minutes.

4. Indicates movement from a larger to a smaller place (e.g., from a train platform into a train, or from the lay world into a religious organization): "in, into."

Note: Contrast with *o* (#18, no. 6).

a) Indicates movement from larger to smaller physical place.

東京駅の前でバスに乗って下さい。

Tōkyō-eki no mae de basu ni notte kudasai.

Please board the bus in front of Tokyo Station.

オフィスに入ったら、タバコは吸わないで下さい。

Ofisu ni haittara, tabako wa suwanai de kudasai.

Please don't smoke after entering the office. / Please don't smoke inside the office.

b) Indicates movement from larger to smaller abstract place.

去年渡辺さんは歴史学会に入った。

Kyonen Watanabe-san wa rekishi-gakkai ni haitta.

Last year Watanabe joined a historical society.

あなたはぼくの夢の中に何度も出てきました。

Anata wa boku no yume no naka ni nando mo dete ki-mashita.

You have appeared in my dreams any number of times.

5. Indicates movement toward a place: "to."

Note: *E* (#14, no. 1) can also be used here.

アメリカに行きたい。

Amerika ni ikitai.

I want to go to America.

ジョンさんは銀行に行きましたよ。

Jon-san wa ginkō ni ikimashita yo.

John went to the bank, you know.

6. Indicates the object of an action: "to."

Note: In this usage, *e* may not be used.

a) Used after a noun. The distinction between this usage and that in no. 5 is that here the noun implies an action (e.g., going shopping, seeing Kabuki).

買い物に行きます。

Kaimono ni ikimasu.

I'm going shopping.

明日は歌舞伎に行くつもりです。

Ashita wa kabuki ni iku tsumori desu.

I plan to go to [see] Kabuki tomorrow.

b) Used after the base of a *-masu* verb.

もうお昼ですから、食事をしに行きませんか。

Mō ohiru desu kara, shokuji o shi ni ikimasen ka.

Since it's noon already, shall we go to eat lunch?

木下さんは友達を迎えに成田まで出かけました。

Kinoshita-san wa tomodachi o mukae ni Narita made deka-kemashita.

Kinoshita went out to Narita [Airport] to meet [pick up] a friend.

7. Indicates the recipient of an action (in English, equivalent to the indirect object): "to, from."

Note: When the meaning is "to," *e* may replace *ni*; when the meaning is "from," *kara* may replace *ni*.

クリスマスには友達にプレゼントをあげる。

Kurisumasu ni wa tomodachi ni purezento o ageru.

We give presents to our friends at Christmas.

クリスマスに友達にプレゼントをもらった。

Kurisumasu ni tomodachi ni purezento o moratta.

I received a present from my friend at Christmas.

昨日フランスにいるナンシーに手紙を出してあげた。

Kinō Furansu ni iru Nanshī ni tegami o dashite ageta.

Yesterday I sent a letter to Nancy in France.

8. Indicates the result of a change or an impending change.

ジョンさんは大学を卒業して、医者になった。

Jon-san wa daigaku o sotsugyō shite, isha ni natta.

John graduated from university and became a doctor.

このケーキを３つに分けて下さい。

Kono kēki o mittsu ni wakete kudasai.

Please divide this cake into three [parts].

渡辺さんは仕事のしすぎで病気になった。

Watanabe-san wa shigoto no shisugi de byōki ni natta.

Watanabe become ill from overwork.

9. Indicates a condition already in existence (usually followed by *natte iru* and equivalent to the English "to be").

この建物の右側が教室になっています。

Kono tatemono no migigawa ga kyōshitsu ni natte imasu.

The right side of this building is a classroom.

ホテルの前がビーチになっています。

Hoteru no mae ga bīchi ni natte imasu.

In front of the hotel is a beach. (Lit., The front of the hotel is a beach.)

10. Indicates the agent of a passive verb (the person or thing performing the action): "by."

電車の中で、すりにお金を取られた。

Densha no naka de, suri ni okane o torareta.

My money was taken by a pickpocket in the train.

家に帰る途中で雨に降られた。

Ie ni kaeru tochū de ame ni furareta.

On my way home I got rained on. (Lit., I was fallen on by the rain.)

11. Indicates the person(s) made to do something in a causative sentence.

先生は学生に漢字を書かせました。

Sensei wa gakusei ni kanji o kakasemashita.

The teacher had the students write *kanji*.

子供たちに本を読ませることはとても大切だ。

Kodomo-tachi ni hon o yomaseru koto wa totemo taisetsu da.

It is very important to have children read books.

12. Indicates the agent of a causative-passive verb (the person or thing performing the action): "by."

学生は先生に漢字を書かされました。

Gakusei wa sensei ni kanji o kakasaremashita.

The students were made to write *kanji* by the teacher.

私は子供のとき、母に嫌いな物も食べさせられました。

Watashi wa kodomo no toki, haha ni kirai na mono mo tabesaseraremashita.

When I was a child, I was made to eat even things I disliked by my mother (my mother made me eat food I didn't like).

*13. Joins nouns (usually three or more): "and."

Note: This usage of *ni* is equivalent to *to* (#6, I-1), but is more commonly found in writing.

その会議に出席した人は、中国人に、韓国人に、日本人だった。

Sono kaigi ni shusseki shita hito wa, Chūgoku-jin ni, Kankoku-jin ni, Nihon-jin datta.

The people attending the conference were Chinese, Koreans, and Japanese.

パーティーの飲物は、日本酒に、ウイスキーに、ワインでした。

Pātī no nomimono wa, Nihon-shu ni, uisukī ni, wain deshita.

The drinks [available] at the party were *sake*, whiskey, and wine.

*14. Indicates a pair of people or things that are commonly mentioned together: "and."

ロメオにジュリエット。

Romeo ni Jurietto.

Romeo and Juliet.

富士山に芸者。

Fuji-san ni geisha.

Mt. Fuji and geisha (a hackneyed phrase in reference to Japan).

*15. Indicates the basis on which, or means by which, an action takes place (usually used with the verbs *motozuku* (to be based on) and *yoru* (owing to).

あの映画は有名な小説に基づいて作られました。

Ano eiga wa yūmei na shōsetsu ni motozuite tsukuraremashita.

That movie was [made] based on a famous novel.

テレビの普及によって、外国の様子がよくわかるようになった。

Terebi no fukyū ni yotte, gaikoku no yōsu ga yoku wakaru yō ni natta.

Thanks to the spread [owing to the spread] of television, we [now] have a better understanding of conditions in foreign countries.

14 — | E | へ

Note: In both of the usages below, *ni* may replace *e*, except when *e* is followed by *no* (as in the last sentence of no. 2).

1. Indicates a direction or goal, or a destination toward which one is moving or at which one has arrived: "to."

いつ京都へ行きますか。

Itsu Kyōto e ikimasu ka.

When are you going to Kyoto?

谷口さんは昨日アメリカへ出発しました。

Taniguchi-san wa kinō Amerika e shuppatsu shimashita.

Taniguchi left for the United States yesterday.

この飛行機は、6時に成田空港へ到着しました。

Kono hikō-ki wa, rokuji ni Narita kūkō e tōchaku shimashita.

This airplane arrived at Narita Airport at six o'clock.

2. Indicates the recipient of an action (in English, equivalent to the indirect object): "to."

外国にいる友達へ手紙を書いた。

Gaikoku ni iru tomodachi e tegami o kaita.

I wrote a letter to a friend abroad.

夕方川田さんへ電話をかけたが、いなかった。

Yūgata Kawada-san e denwa o kaketa ga, inakatta.

I telephoned Kawada in the evening, but he wasn't there.

川田さんへの電話があったのは何時でしたか。

Kawada-san e no denwa ga atta no wa nanji deshita ka.

What time did that phone call come for Kawada?

15 — | KARA | から

I. Follows nouns and the *-te* form of verbs: "from."

1. After nouns, indicates the time at which something begins: "from, at."

銀行は9時から開いています。

*Ginkō wa kuji **kara** aite imasu.*

Banks are open from nine o'clock. / Banks open at nine.

日本語のクラスは、1時から4時までです。

*Nihon-go no kurasu wa, ichiji **kara** yoji made desu.*

Japanese class lasts from one to four o'clock.

2. After nouns, indicates the place from which something begins: "from, at."

マラソンはここから出発します。

*Marason wa koko **kara** shuppatsu shimasu.*

The marathon starts [from] here.

社長はパリから飛行機でスペインへ行きます。

*Shachō wa Pari **kara** hikō-ki de Supein e ikimasu.*

The company president will go from Paris to Spain by plane.

*3. Certain idiomatic usages in which figurative references to place are made.

新聞をすみからすみまで読んだ。

*Shinbun o sumi **kara** sumi made yonda.*

I read the newspaper from beginning to end. (Lit., . . . from corner to corner.)

女の人の目から見れば、日本にはまだ差別がたくさんある。

*Onna no hito no me **kara** mireba, Nihon ni wa mada sabetsu ga takusan aru.*

From a woman's viewpoint, there is still a lot of discrimination in Japan. (Lit., Looking from a woman's eyes . . .)

4. After the *-te* form of verbs, indicates that an action begins immediately after the previous one ends: "after."

昨日私は仕事が終わってから買物をしました。

*Kinō watashi wa shigoto ga owatte **kara** kaimono o shimashita.*

Yesterday I went shopping after finishing work.

明日の夜、食事をしてから映画を見ませんか。

*Ashita no yoru, shokuji o shite **kara** eiga o mimasen ka.*

How about seeing a movie tomorrow night after [having] dinner?

5. After the *-te* form of verbs, indicates the passage of time: ''since, for.''

山田さんが大学を卒業してから5年になります。

*Yamada-san ga daigaku o sotsugyō shite **kara** gonen ni narimasu.*

Five years have passed since Yamada graduated from college.

あの2人が結婚してから20年だそうです。

*Ano futari ga kekkon shite **kara** nijū-nen da sō desu.*

I understand that it is twenty years since those two were married. / I hear that those two have been married for twenty years.

6. Indicates materials used: ''from.''

Note: *Kara* and *de* (#12, no. 3) are similar in usage. However, the former tends to accompany materials that are the result of a somewhat complex process, whereas the latter is generally used with materials that retain, or appear to retain, their original state, such as wood, rock, leather, paper, and glass.

ワインはぶどうから作ります。

*Wain wa budō **kara** tsukurimasu.*

Wine is made from grapes.

豆腐は何から作るか知っていますか。

*Tōfu wa nani **kara** tsukuru ka shitte imasu ka.*

Do you know what tofu is made from?

7. Indicates the agent of a passive verb (the person or thing performing the action): ''by.''

Note: The agent of a passive verb is usually indicated by *ni*, but *kara* may replace *ni*, with no basic change in meaning, when (1) the noun preceding *kara* can be perceived more as the source of an action than as its agent and (2) when *kara* makes the meaning clearer by avoiding a repetition of *ni* (as in the first example below). Examples of other verbs in conjunction with which *kara* can replace *ni* are *ai suru* (to love), *kiku* (to ask), *meirei suru* (to order), *shikaru* (to scold), *shiraberu* (to examine).

私は大使からパーティーに招待されました。

Watashi wa taishi kara pātī ni shōtai saremashita.

I was invited to a party by the ambassador.

昨日課長から叱られた。

Kinō kachō kara shikarareta.

I was scolded by the section chief yesterday.

II. Follows verbs and adjectives to indicate a cause or reason: "since, because."

1. Indicates a cause or reason: "since, because."

Note: *Kara* can be replaced by *no de* (#26) in this usage. In general, (1) *kara* indicates a more subjective reason, *no de* a more objective one; and (2) *no de* is softer and more polite than *kara*.

忙しかったから私たちは公園へ行きませんでした。

Isogashikatta kara watashi-tachi wa kōen e ikimasen deshita.

We didn't go to the park because we were too busy.

あのレストランは安いからいつも混んでいます。

Ano resutoran wa yasui kara itsu mo konde imasu.

That restaurant is inexpensive, so it's always crowded.

*2. Used trailingly at the end of a sentence, indicates censure or warning to the listener: "so you had better."

そんなことばかり言っているとみんなに嫌われるから
……

Sonna koto bakari itte iru to minna ni kirawareru kara . . .

If you say only those kinds of things, you're going to be disliked by everyone [so stop saying them]. / If you keep saying things like that, people aren't going to like it.

勉強しないと試験に合格できないから……

Benkyō shinai to shiken ni gōkaku dekinai kara . . .

If you don't study, you won't be able to pass the exam [so you had better study].

16 — | MADE | まで

1. Indicates a time limitation for actions or events (often paired with *kara*): "until, till, to."

この会社の社員は9時から5時まで働きます。

Kono kaisha no shain wa kuji kara goji made hatarakimasu.

The employees of this company work from nine o'clock till five o'clock.

このデパートは、土曜日と日曜日は8時までです。

Kono depāto wa, doyōbi to nichiyōbi wa hachiji made desu.

This department store is open until eight o'clock on Saturdays and Sundays.

2. Indicates the place to which an action extends (often paired with *kara*): "to."

この飛行機は東京からホノルルまで行きます。

Kono hikō-ki wa Tōkyō kara Honoruru made ikimasu.

This plane goes from Tokyo to Honolulu.

ここから京都まで何時間かかりますか。

Koko kara Kyōto made nan-jikan kakarimasu ka.

How long does it take to get from here to Kyoto?

3. Indicates the degree of a condition by citing an example (e.g., it is not just cold, it is so cold that my glasses have frozen over): "even, so . . . that."

子供だけでなく大人まで、そのゲームを楽しんだ。

Kodomo dake de naku otona made, sono gēmu o tanoshinda.

Not only the children but even the adults enjoyed [playing] that game.

その日山の上はとても寒くて、夕方には雪まで降って
きた。

*Sono hi yama no ue wa totemo samukute, yūgata ni wa yuki
made futte kita.*

The top of the mountain was very cold that day; it even
started snowing in the evening. / The mountaintop was so
cold that day that it even started to snow in the evening.

*4. Indicates an extreme condition.

斉藤さんは、あの男の人と結婚できなければ死のうと
まで思いつめたそうです。

*Saitō-san wa, ano otoko no hito to kekkon dekinakereba
shinō to made omoitsumeta sō desu.*

Saito was apparently even contemplating suicide if she were
unable to marry the man.

その両親は子供の病気が治るなら、全財産を捨てても
いいとまで考えていた。

*Sono ryōshin wa kodomo no byōki ga naoru nara, zen-zaisan
o sutete mo ii to made kangaete ita.*

If their child would only get well, the parents thought that
they would even sacrifice all they owned. / The child's parents
were [even] prepared to sacrifice all they owned if only he/she
would recover.

***5. At the end of a sentence, indicates a limitation or ex-
tent: "that is all."**

今日はここまで。

Kyō wa koko made.

That's all for today. (Lit., As for today, up to here.)

とりあえずご報告まで。

Toriaezu gohōkoku made.

For your reference. (Lit., For the moment, as far as a report.)

***6. In the form *made mo nai* (which follows verb roots),
emphasizes extent or degree; the complete phrase may
be translated: "there is no need to."**

明日のパーティーにはわざわざ行くまでもない。

*Ashita no pāt̄ ni wa wazawaza iku **made** mo nai.*

There is no need to go out of one's way [to make a special effort] to attend tomorrow's party. / Tomorrow's party is hardly worth going to.

言うまでもないことですが、この会社の経営状態は、かなり悪化しています。

*Iu **made** mo nai koto desu ga, kono kaisha no keiei-jōtai wa, kanari akka shite imasu.*

Needless to say [it goes without saying that], this company's operations have deteriorated considerably.

17 — NO の

I. Used between two nouns, indicating that the first possesses or is modifying the second; also used in place of *ga* to indicate the subject in modifying clauses.

1. Indicates possession: "'s."

これは高木さんの傘です。

*Kore wa Takagi-san **no** kasa desu.*

This is Takagi's umbrella.

それが佐藤さんの車です。

*Sore ga Satō-san **no** kuruma desu.*

That is Satō's car.

Note: If the context is understood, the second noun can be omitted:

それが佐藤さんのです。

*Sore ga Satō-san **no** desu.*

That is Satō's.

2. Indicates position or location.

机の上、いすの下、学校の前、この建物の後ろ。

*Tsukue **no** ue, isu **no** shita, gakkō **no** mae, kono tatemono **no** ushiro.*

The top of the desk [i.e., on the desk]; under the chair; the [area in] front of the school; behind this building.

3. Indicates that the first noun is modifying the second in terms of kind or category.

山田先生は英語の先生です。

Yamada-sensei wa Eigo no sensei desu.

Yamada is a teacher of English [an English teacher].

この学校は料理の学校です。

Kono gakkō wa ryōri no gakkō desu.

This school is a cooking school.

4. Indicates that two nouns are in apposition.

K大学学長の今井氏が演説をしています。

K daigaku gakuchō no Imai-shi ga enzetsu o shite imasu.

Mr. Imai, the president of K University, is making a speech.

こちらが佐山さんのお姉さんの千香子さんです。

Kochira ga Sayama-san no onēsan no Chikako-san desu.

This is Chikako, Sayama's elder sister.

5. Used to replace *ga* to indicate the subject of a clause modifying a noun.

これは坂本さんの描いた油絵です。

Kore wa Sakamoto-san no kaita aburae desu.

This is the oil painting that Sakamoto painted.

昨日あなたの話していたレストランはどこですか。

Kinō anata no hanashite ita resutoran wa doko desu ka.

Where is the restaurant you were talking about yesterday?

II. Used to nominalize verbs and adjectives.

1. Simple nominalizer: "-ing, what."

天気が悪いですから、ドライブに行くのはやめましょう。

Tenki ga warui desu kara, doraibu ni iku no wa yamemashō.

Since the weather is bad, let's call off going for a drive.

外国語を学ぶのは、むずかしいですね。

Gaikoku-go o manabu no wa, muzukashii desu ne.

Learning a foreign language is difficult, isn't it.

彼女が欲しいのは、新しいピアノです。

Kanojo ga hoshii no wa, atarashii piano desu.

What she wants is a new piano.

2. Used as a nominalizer before verbs of perception (e.g., *mieru* [to be visible], *kikoeru* [to be audible]).

このビルの屋上から、車が走っているのがよく見えます。

Kono biru no okujō kara, kuruma ga hashitte iru no ga yoku miemasu.

From the roof [top] of this building, you can clearly see the cars going by. (Lit., . . . the driving cars are easily visible.)

女の人が歌っているのが聞こえますね。

Onna no hito ga utatte iru no ga kikoemasu ne.

You can hear a woman singing, can't you. (Lit., A woman's singing is audible . . .)

III. Used at the end of sentences.

1. Indicates a question (colloquial usage).

会社、本当にやめるの。

Kaisha, hontō ni yameru no.

You really quitting the company?

明日は何時に出かけるの。

Ashita wa nanji ni dekakeru no.

What time you leaving tomorrow?

2. Imparts a softer tone to a statement (usually used by women).

私、来月フランスに留学するの。

Watashi, raigetsu Furansu ni ryūgaku suru no.

I will be going to France to study next month.

土曜日はコンサートに行きたいと思っているの。

Doyōbi wa konsāto ni ikitai to omotte iru no.

I'm thinking I'd like to go to a concert on Saturday.

*3. Indicates a mild command.

そんなこといわないの。

Sonna koto iwanai no.

Don't say such things. / Don't say that.

あなたは黙っていればいいの。

Anata wa damatte ireba ii no.

You just keep quiet. (Lit., As for you, if you keep silent, it's good.)

18 — O | を

1. Indicates the object of an action (direct object).

夕べは映画を見た。

Yūbe wa eiga o mita.

I saw a movie yesterday evening.

原田さんは手紙を書いている。

Harada-san wa tegami o kaite iru.

Harada is writing a letter.

2. Indicates the direct object of a passive verb.

私は昨日、電車の中でお金とパスポートを盗まれました。

Watashi wa kinō, densha no naka de okane to pasupōto o nusumaremashita.

I had my money and passport stolen in the train yesterday.

彼女は犬に手を嚙まれた。

Kanojo wa inu ni te o kamareta.

She had her hand bitten by a dog.

3. Indicates the person or thing made to do something in a causative sentence.

その政治家は、財界人のパーティーに秘書を出席させた。

Sono seiji-ka wa, zaikai-jin no pātī ni hisho o shusseki saseta.

That politician had her secretary attend a business leaders' party.

部長は部下を出張させた。

Buchō wa buka o shutchō saseta.

The department head sent a subordinate on a business trip.

4. Indicates a specific occupation or position (usually followed by *suru*).

山本さんのお父さんは、医者をしている。

Yamamoto-san no otōsan wa, isha o shite iru.

Yamamoto's father is a physician.

私の兄は、新聞記者をしています。

Watashi no ani wa, shinbun-kisha o shite imasu.

My elder brother is a newspaper reporter.

5. Used with verbs indicating wishes or desires ending in *-tai* or *-tagaru*.

Note: *Ga* (#2, I-12) can replace *o* in this usage, but lends a slightly stronger emphasis.

コーヒーを飲みたいんです。

Kōhī o nomitai-n desu.

I want to drink some coffee.

ジョンさんはおすしを食べたがっていますよ。

Jon-san wa osushi o tabetagatte imasu yo.

John feels like eating some sushi.

6. Indicates movement from a smaller to a larger place in both concrete and abstract senses.

Note: (1) Contrast with *ni* (#13, no. 4). (2) Although *kara* sounds correct from the standpoint of English, it should not be substituted for *o* in this usage.

a) Movement from a smaller physical space to a larger physical place (with the larger place usually implicit).

毎日新宿駅で地下鉄を降ります。

Mainichi Shinjuku-eki de chikatetsu o orimasu.

I get off the subway at Shinjuku Station every day.

山本さんは夕方5時半に会社を出ます。

Yamamoto-san wa yūgata goji-han ni kaisha o demasu.

Yamamoto leaves the office at 5:30 in the evening.

b) Movement from a smaller space in an abstract sense to a larger abstract space (e.g., from school life into society at large).

首相は早稲田大学を卒業した。

Shushō wa Waseda daigaku o sotsugyō shita.

The prime minister graduated from Waseda University.

沖氏は、70歳になった年に経済界を引退した。

Oki-shi wa, nanajussai ni natta toshi ni keizai-kai o intai shita.

Mr. Oki retired from the business world when [in the year in which] he turned seventy.

7. When used with verbs of motion, indicates the place of the motion.

車で新しい橋を渡った。

Kuruma de atarashii hashi o watatta.

I crossed over the new bridge by car.

私の国では、車は道の左側を走ります。

Watashi no kuni de wa, kuruma wa michi no hidarigawa o hashirimasu.

In my country, cars drive on the left side of the road.

このバスは、デパートの前を通りますか。

Kono basu wa, depāto no mae o tōrimasu ka.

Does this bus pass in front of the department store?

8. Indicates the starting point of an action.

社長は火曜日の午後6時に成田を出発します。

*Shachō wa kayōbi no gogo rokuji ni Narita **o** shuppatsu shimasu.*

The company president will leave from Narita at 6 P.M. on Tuesday.

この電車は8時に東京駅を出ますから遅れないで来て
下さい。

*Kono densha wa hachiji ni Tōkyō-eki **o** demasu kara okurenaide kite kudasai.*

This train leaves Tokyo Station at eight o'clock, so please don't be late.

19 — ## KURAI (GURAI)
くらい（ぐらい）

1. Indicates an approximate amount or extent; in contrast with *hodo* and *bakari*, *kurai* denotes an approximate quantity without connoting its upper or lower limits: "approximately, about."

Note: *Hodo* (#20, no. 1) and *bakari* (#21, no. 1) may replace *kurai* in this usage.

ここからその学校まで車で30分ぐらいかかります。

*Koko kara sono gakkō made kuruma de sanjippun **gurai** kakarimasu.*

It takes about thirty minutes by car to get to the school from here.

昨日のパーティーに来た人は、100人ぐらいだったと
思います。

*Kinō no pātī ni kita hito wa, hyakunin **gurai** datta to omoimasu.*

I think about 100 people came to the party yesterday.

2. Indicates the extent of an action or condition after a specific example is given: "so ... that, to the extent that."

Note: *Hodo* (#20, no. 3) may replace *kurai/gurai* in this usage.

安田さんの旅行の話は面白くて、時間のたつのも忘れたくらいだった。

*Yasuda-san no ryokō no hanashi wa omoshirokute, jikan no tatsu no mo wasureta **kurai** datta.*

Yasuda's stories of her trip were so interesting that we lost track of time.

恥ずかしくて穴があったら入りたいぐらいだった。

*Hazukashikute ana ga attara hairitai **gurai** datta.*

I was so embarrassed that I felt like crawling in a hole. (Lit., . . . if there had been a hole, I would have wanted to go in it.)

3. Indicates a comparison: "as . . . as."

Note: *Hodo* (#20, no.2) may replace *kurai/gurai* in this usage.

山下さんの新しい家の庭は、ゴルフ場くらいの大きさだ。

*Yamashita-san no atarashii ie no niwa wa, gorufu-jō **gurai** no ōkisa da.*

The garden at Yamashita's new house is as big as a golf course.

自分の家くらい、いい場所はない。

*Jibun no ie **kurai**, ii basho wa nai.*

There's no place as nice as one's own home.

20 — | HODO | ほど

1. Indicates an approximate amount or approximate maximum extent; in contrast with *kurai* and *bakari*, *hodo* tends to stress approximate upper limit: "approximately, about."

Note: *Kurai* (#19, no. 1) and *bakari* (#21, no. 1) may replace *hodo* in this usage, although *hodo* is somewhat more formal.

来月は、一週間ほど九州へ出張します。

*Raigetsu wa, isshūkan **hodo** Kyūshū e shutchō shimasu.*

Next month I'll be going on a business trip to Kyushu for as long as a week.

今度の事故で、100人ほどの人が死んだそうです。

*Kondo no jiko de, hyakunin **hodo** no hito ga shinda sō desu.*

I hear that some 100 people died in this traffic accident.

2. Indicates a comparison (used only in negative sentences): "as . . . as."

Note: *Kurai* may replace *hodo* in this usage, but *hodo* is more common.

今年は去年ほど寒くないです。

*Kotoshi wa kyonen **hodo** samuku nai desu.*

This year is not as cold as last year.

あの人ほど頭のいい人はいないでしょう。

*Ano hito **hodo** atama no ii hito wa inai deshō.*

No one has as good a head as he has. / No one is as smart as he is.

3. Indicates the extent of an action or condition by citing an specific example: "so . . . that, to the extent that."

Note: This usage is similar to *kurai* (#19, no. 2).

今日は勉強ができないほど疲れた。

*Kyō wa benkyō ga dekinai **hodo** tsukareta.*

Today I'm so tired that I can't study.

試験に合格したので、うれしくて眠れないほどです。

*Shiken ni gōkaku shita no de, ureshikute nemurenai **hodo** desu.*

Since I passed the examination, I'm so happy that I can't sleep.

4. Used in the form V-*ba* + V *hodo*: "the more . . . the more."

北へ行けば行く**ほど**寒くなります。

*Kita e ikeba iku **hodo** samuku narimasu.*

The further north you go, the colder it gets.

年をとればとる**ほど**、体が弱くなります。

*Toshi o toreba toru **hodo**, karada ga yowaku narimasu.*

The older you get, the weaker your body becomes.

21 — | BAKARI | ばかり |

Note: More informal forms of *bakari* are *bakkari*, *bakashi*, and *bak-kashi*.

1. Indicates an approximate amount or extent; in contrast to *kurai* and *hodo*, *bakari* tends (but only tends) to focus on the smallness of the amount: "approximately, about."

Note: *Kurai* (#19, no. 1) and *hodo* (#20, no. 1) may replace *bakari* in this usage.

明日から2日**ばかり**旅行に行ってきます。

*Ashita kara futsuka **bakari** ryokō ni itte kimasu.*

Beginning tomorrow, I'll be making a trip for a day or two. / Tomorrow I'll be leaving on a trip for a couple of days.

1万円**ばかり**貸していただけませんか。

*Ichi-man-en **bakari** kashite itadakemasen ka.*

Could you lend me, say, something like ¥10,000?

2. "Not only . . . but also."

Note: While *dake* (#22, no. 4) may replace *bakari* in this usage, *bakari* is slightly more emphatic.

原田さんはピアノ**ばかり**でなく、歌もうまいんですよ。

Harada-san wa piano **bakari** *de naku, uta mo umai-n desu yo.*

Harada is good not only at the piano but also at singing.

英語ばかりでなく、フランス語も勉強したいんです。

Eigo bakari de naku, Furansu-go mo benkyō shitai-n desu.

I want to study not only English but French as well.

3. Emphasizes the singularity of the immediately preceding word: "only, nothing but."

Note: (1) Since the position of *bakari* in the sentence affects the meaning, several versions of one sentence have been given to exemplify the difference. In loose usage, however, *bakari* tends to shift from the word it is intended to modify, leaving the meaning to be gathered from context. (2) In this usage, *bakari* contains a degree of disapproval which *dake* does not.

課長はこの頃ウイスキーばかり飲んでいますね。

Kachō wa konogoro uisukī **bakari** *nonde imasu ne.*

The section chief is drinking nothing but whiskey these days.

課長はこの頃ウイスキーを飲んでばかりいますね。

Kachō wa konogoro uisukī o nonde **bakari** *imasu ne.*

The section chief is doing nothing but drink whiskey these days.

課長はこの頃ウイスキーを飲んでいるばかりですね。

Kachō wa konogoro uisukī o nonde iru **bakari** *desu ne.*

All the section chief does these days is drink whiskey.

テレビばかり見ていると目を悪くしますよ。

Terebi **bakari** *mite iru to me o waruku shimasu yo.*

If all you do is watch TV, you'll ruin your eyes. / If you watch TV all the time, you'll ruin your eyes.

Note: Here, *terebi o mite iru bakari da to me o waruku shimasu yo* is also possible (and grammatically more acceptable), but the example above is more common and has the same meaning.

4. Used after the *-ta* form of verbs: "just."

Note: If *tokoro* (#38, no. 1) replaces *bakari* in this usage, the meaning is similar, but *bakari* shows more emphasis.

父は今帰ってきたばかりです。

*Chichi wa ima kaette kita **bakari** desu.*

My father just now came home [just got home].

順ちゃんは、ご飯を食べた**ばかり**なのに、もうおやつ
を欲しがっています。

*Jun-chan wa, gohan o tabeta **bakari** na no ni, mō oyatsu o hoshigatte imasu.*

Even though Jun has just eaten a meal [just finished eating], he already wants a snack.

*5. Emphasizes a reason or cause in the phrase *bakari ni*: ''(just, merely) because, for the simple reason.''

渡辺さんはステレオを買いたい**ばかり**に、一生懸命に
アルバイトをしている。

*Watanabe-san wa sutereo o kaitai **bakari** ni, isshō-kenmei ni arubaito o shite iru.*

Watanabe is working like a dog at his part-time job for the simple reason that he wants to buy a stereo. / Watanabe wants to buy a stereo so badly that he is working for all he's worth at his part-time job.

山田さんは政治家と結婚した**ばかり**に、苦労してい
る。

*Yamada-san wa seiji-ka to kekkon shita **bakari** ni, kurō shite iru.*

Simply because Yamada married a politician, she is having a hard time. / Just because she married [happened to marry] a politician, Yamada is finding the going tough.

22 — | DAKE | だけ

1. Indicates an absolute quantitative limit with the connotation that the amount is small: ''only, just.''

昨日クラスに来た学生は、5人**だけ**でした。

*Kinō kurasu ni kita gakusei wa, gonin **dake** deshita.*

Only five students came to class yesterday.

今日は1時間だけテレビを見ました。

*Kyō wa ichi-jikan **dake** terebi o mimashita.*

Today I watched TV for only an hour.

2. Indicates an extent or amount: "as . . . as."

どうぞお好きなだけお飲み下さい。

*Dōzo osuki na **dake** onomi kudasai.*

Please drink as much as you wish.

できるだけ早く行きます。

*Dekiru **dake** hayaku ikimasu.*

I'll go [be on my way, leave, get there] as soon as I can. (Lit., To the extent that I can, I will go quickly.)

*3. In the phrases *dake ni*, *dake atte*, and *dake no koto wa aru*, indicates the cause or precondition for a certain result or state of affairs (when the result meets expectations, does not meet expectations, or is considered a natural outcome).

a) When the result meets expectations and is therefore worth the effort of achieving: ". . . was worthwhile."

あの大学に合格できたから、勉強しただけのことはあった。

*Ano daigaku ni gōkaku dekita kara, benkyō shita **dake** no koto wa atta.*

I passed [the entrance examination to] that university, so the studying I did was worth it.

寺田さんは私のプレゼントを喜んでくれたので、無理して買っただけのことはあった。

*Terada-san wa watashi no purezento o yorokonde kureta no de, muri shite katta **dake** no koto wa atta.*

Since Terada was happy [pleased] with my present, it was worth all the trouble I went to in buying it.

b) When the result does not meet expectations and is therefore discouraging: "given the fact that."

彼は彼女に夢中だっただけに、失恋のショックはとても大きかった。

*Kare wa kanojo ni muchū datta **dake** ni, shitsuren no shokku wa totemo ōkikatta.*

Given the fact that he was head over heels in love, losing her was a big blow.

一生懸命に勉強しただけに、不合格の通知を受け取ったとき、山本さんは非常にがっかりした。

*Isshō-kenmei ni benkyō shita **dake** ni, fu-gōkaku no tsūchi o uketotta toki, Yamamoto-san wa hijō ni gakkari shita.*

Since he had studied so hard, Yamamoto was extremely disappointed when he received notification that he had failed. / Given the fact that he had studied so hard, Yamamoto was crushed when he learned that he had not been accepted.

c) When the outcome is seen as a natural result of foregoing conditions: ''as you might expect.''

佐藤さんは英国の大学で勉強しただけあって、英語がうまいですね。

*Satō-san wa Eikoku no daigaku de benkyō shita **dake** atte, Eigo ga umai desu ne.*

As you might expect from his having studied at a university in England, Sato's English is quite good.

ジョンさんは、京都に15年も住んでいるだけあって、お寺のことをよく知っています。

*Jon-san wa, Kyōto ni jūgo-nen mo sunde iru **dake** atte, otera no koto o yoku shitte imasu.*

As you might expect from his having lived in Kyoto for fifteen years, John is very knowledgeable about temples. / Since John has lived in Kyoto for fifteen years, it is not surprising that he knows a lot about temples.

一流のピアニストだけに、すばらしい演奏をしますね。

*Ichiryū no pianisuto **dake** ni, subarashii ensō o shimasu ne.*

As you might expect of a first-rate pianist, he plays wonderfully, doesn't he.

ここは北海道だけに、寒さが厳しいです。

*Koko wa Hokkaidō **dake** ni, samusa ga kibishii desu.*

As you might expect from this being Hokkaido, it is terribly cold. / It is terribly cold here in Hokkaido, as you might expect.

4. "Not only . . . but also."

Note: While *bakari* (#21, no. 2) may replace *dake* in this usage, it is slightly more emphatic.

原田さんはピアノだけでなく、歌もうまいんですよ。

*Harada-san wa piano **dake** de naku, uta mo umai-n desu yo.*

Harada is good not only at the piano but also at singing.

英語だけでなくフランス語も勉強したいんです。

*Eigo **dake** de naku Furansu-go mo benkyō shitai-n desu.*

I want to study not only English but French as well.

23 — SHIKA | しか

Note: *Shika* is used only with negative verbs. It may combine with (follow) *dake*, *nomi*, and *kiri* for further emphasis.

1. After nouns, indicates there is nothing more than the quantity specified, with the connotation that the quantity is small or unsatisfactory: "only, nothing but, merely."

あの店には、この雑誌しかありませんでした。

*Ano mise ni wa, kono zasshi **shika** arimasen deshita.*

This was the only magazine at that store. / The only magazine that store had was this one.

今は、1300円きりしか持っていないから、とてもフランス料理など食べられないよ。

*Ima wa, sen-sanbyaku-en kiri **shika** motte inai kara, totemo Furansu-ryōri nado taberarenai yo.*

Since all I have at the moment is ¥1,300, there is no way I can [afford to] eat French food.

*2. After verbs, indicates a limiting to the action stipulated by the verb: "there is no choice but, all one can do is."

いやだけれど、出張だから行く**しかない**。

*Iya da keredo, shutchō da kara iku **shika nai**.*

I don't want to, but since it's company business [lit., a business trip], I can't help but go [I have no choice].

このレポートは、明日までだから、今日中に終わらせる**しかない**。

*Kono repōto wa, ashita made da kara, kyō-jū ni owaraseru **shika nai**.*

Since this report is due tomorrow, I have no choice but to finish it sometime today [will just to have to finish it sometime today].

24 — | NOMI | のみ

*1. After nouns, indicates that there is nothing other than the thing(s) stipulated: "only."

Note: In this usage, *nomi* and *dake* have the same meaning, but *nomi* is used more in writing than in the spoken language. *Nomi* can be combined with (followed by) *shika*, as in the second sample sentence below.

この会議には、4つの国の代表**のみ**が出席した。

*Kono kaigi ni wa, yottsu no kuni no daihyō **nomi** ga shusseki shita.*

The representatives of only four countries attended this conference.

以前、この大学には男性**のみ**しか入れなかった。

*Izen, kono daigaku ni wa dansei **nomi** shika hairenakatta.*

In the past, only men were able to enter this university.

*2. Used in the form *A nomi narazu B mo*: "not only . . . but also."

Note: This usage is essentially equivalent to *bakari* (#21, no. 2) and *dake* (#22, no. 4), but is found more in the written than in the spoken language.

この大学の文学部の学生は、英語**のみ**ならずフランス

語も勉強しなければならない。

Kono daigaku no bungaku-bu no gakusei wa, Eigo nomi narazu Furansu-go mo benkyō shinakereba naranai.

The students in the literature department of this university must study not only English, but French as well.

シェークスピアは戯曲の**み**ならず詩もたくさん書いた。

*Shēkusupia wa gikyoku **nomi** narazu shi mo takusan kaita.*

Shakespeare wrote not only plays, but many poems as well.

25 — KIRI | きり

1. Used after nouns and verbs, indicates a "cutting-off" point, i.e., a limit; may also be pronounced *kkiri* (っきり): "only."

Note: *Kiri* means basically the same thing as *dake* (#22, no. 1) but is a more colloquial usage. *Shika* may be used after *kiri* for emphasis.

あのおじいさんは、１人**きり**で大きな家に住んでいる。

*Ano ojī-san wa, hitori **kiri** de ōki na ie ni sunde iru.*

That old man lives alone [all by himself] in a big house.

その子供は、黙った**きり**で何も言わなかった。

*Sono kodomo wa, damatta **kiri** de nani mo iwanakatta.*

The child just sat [stood, etc.] there, without saying a word. (Lit., That child, only keeping quiet, didn't say anything.)

2. Used with a small number or amount to emphasize a negative meaning; *dake* may replace *kiri*: "only."

あと発車まで２分**きり**だから、山本さんはとても間に合わないだろう。

*Ato hassha made nifun **kiri** da kara, Yamamoto-san wa totemo ma-ni-awanai darō.*

The train leaves in just two minutes, so it's very unlikely that Yamamoto will make it in time.

お金は1万円きりしかないから、あのコンピューターを買うのは無理だ。

Okane wa ichiman-en kiri shika nai kara, ano konpyūtā o kau no wa muri da.

I have only ¥10,000 to my name, so there's no way I can buy that computer. / Since all I have is ¥10,000, there is no way I can afford that computer.

3. Indicates the most recent incidence of something: "the last."

アランさんからは、去年クリスマス・カードが来たきりで、そのあと手紙が来ません。

Aran-san kara wa, kyonen kurisumasu-kādo ga kita kiri de, sono ato tegami ga kimasen.

The last [I heard] from Allen was a Christmas card last year; since then, no letters have come.

岸さんとは、先月のクラス会で会ったきりです。

Kishi-san to wa, sengetsu no kurasu kai de atta kiri desu.

The last [time] I saw Kishi was at last month's class meeting.

26 — NO DE | ので

1. Indicates a cause or reason: "in that, since, because."

Note: *No de* and *kara* (#15, II-1) differ in two ways: first, *no de* usually indicates a more objective cause or reason, *kara* a more subjective one; thus *kara* is often used in sentences involving prohibitions, commands, and questions; second, in sentences otherwise identical, *no de* lends a more polite tone.

車の事故があったので、道が混んでいます。

Kuruma no jiko ga atta no de, michi ga konde imasu.

Since there was a car accident, the roads are crowded.

雪がたくさん降ったので、電車が遅れるそうです。

*Yuki ga takusan futta **no de**, densha ga okureru sō desu.*

Because a lot of snow has fallen, it is said [they say, I hear] the train is going to be late. / Because of all the snow, the train will be late, I hear.

病気なので、旅行に行くのは無理です。

*Byōki na **no de**, ryokō ni iku no wa muri desu.*

Since I'm ill, taking a trip is out of the question.

Note: As in this example, *da* changes to *na* before *no de*.

---

27 — | MONO DE | もので |

---

1. Indicates a cause or reason: "in that, inasmuch as, given."

Note: *Mono de* is more polite and formal than *no de* and *kara*.

東京は物価が高いもので、生活が大変です。

*Tōkyō wa bukka ga takai **mono de**, seikatsu ga taihen desu.*

Since prices are high, life in Tokyo is difficult. / Prices in Tokyo being high, it is difficult to make ends meet.

私は体が弱いもので、長い旅行は無理です。

*Watashi wa karada ga yowai **mono de**, nagai ryokō wa muri desu.*

In that my constitution is weak [health is poor], long trips are out of the question.

---

28 — | KEREDOMO | けれども |

Note: (1) More colloquial forms of *keredomo* are *keredo*, *kedo*, and *kedomo*. *Keredomo* in all its forms lends a softer tone, and in its full form (not the alternative forms) tends to be preceded by *desu* and the *-masu* verb forms. (2) In each of the usages below, *ga* (#2, II-1, 2, 4, 5, 6) can replace *keredomo* and its more informal variations.

1. Used between two clauses to indicate that they are opposed in meaning: "but, although."

天気予報で今日は雨は降らないと言ったんですけれども、夕方から降ってきましたね。

*Tenki-yohō de kyō wa ame wa furanai to itta-n desu **keredomo**, yūgata kara futte kimashita ne.*

They said on the weather report that it wouldn't rain today, but it began raining in the evening, didn't it.

竹内さんに電話をかけたけれど留守でした。

*Takeuchi-san ni denwa o kaketa **keredo** rusu deshita.*

I called Takeuchi, but she was out.

2. Used at the end of a sentence, implies something that qualifies what is actually stated: "well, yes, but . . ."

Note: This usage is essentially the same as that in no. 1, above, except that here the second clause isn't stated outright. (Words in brackets below show only one of various imaginable contexts.)

たまには旅行にも行きたいと思っているんですけど……

*Tama ni wa ryokō ni mo ikitai to omotte iru-n desu **kedo** . . .*

I'd really like to go on a trip once in a while . . . [but I don't have the time].

私はゴルフをしないわけではないんですけど……

*Watashi wa gorufu o shinai wake de wa nai-n desu **kedo** . . .*

It's not that I don't play golf . . . [but I really don't like it that much].

3. Indicates a preliminary remark.

まだ発車まで1時間もありますけど、どうしましょうか。

*Mada hassha made ichi-jikan mo arimasu **kedo**, dō shimashō ka.*

There's still an hour until [the train] departs, [so] what shall we do [in the meanwhile]?

谷ですけど、知子さんいらっしゃいますか。

*Tani desu **kedo**, Tomoko-san irasshaimasu ka.*

This [my name is] is Tani. Is Tomoko there?

4. Used at the end of a sentence, emphasizes the sense that the speaker wants the event to come out as stated: "it would be nice if, I hope."

早く暖かくなるといいんだけど……

Hayaku atatakaku naru to ii-n da kedo . . .

It would be nice if it got warm soon. / I hope it gets warm soon.

もう少し大きいのが欲しいんだけれど……

Mō sukoshi ōkii no ga hoshii-n da keredo . . .

I'd like to have one that's a little bigger. / I had hoped for something a little larger.

29 — | TOKORO DE | ところで

Note: *Tokoro de* is always used after the *-ta* form of a verb. The tense of this verb, however, is not necessarily past, but is determined by the tense of the verb in the main clause.

*1. Between contrasting clauses, emphasizes that an extent, number, or amount of something is less than expected: "even if, even though."

Note: This usage is similar to *-te mo* (#4, no. 1), but the emphasis is greater with *tokoro de*.

東京は雪が降ったところで、そんなに積もることはありません。

Tōkyō wa yuki ga futta tokoro de, sonna ni tsumoru koto wa arimasen.

Even though it snows in Tokyo, it never snows that much [never gets that deep].

あの人ならいくら頑張ったところで、この程度の仕事しかできないでしょう。

Ano hito nara ikura ganbatta tokoro de, kono teido no shigoto shika dekinai deshō.

Try as he might, this is about the best [level of work] he can do.

*2. Indicates that the outcome of what is stated in the first clause will not be favorable: "Even if, no matter how much."

今から急いで行ったところで、1時の新幹線には間に合いませんよ。

Ima kara isoide itta tokoro de, ichiji no shinkansen ni wa ma-ni-aimasen yo.

No matter how much we hurry now, we're just not going to be on time for the one o'clock Shinkansen.

高岡さんに頼んだところで、やってくれるはずがないでしょう。

Takaoka-san ni tanonda tokoro de, yatte kureru hazu ga nai deshō.

Even if we asked Takaoka, there's little chance he would do it for us.

30 — NO NI のに

1. Used between two clauses to indicate that they are opposed in meaning: "although, even though, despite the fact that."

Note: *No ni* indicates a stronger opposition in meaning than *ga* (#2, II-1) or *keredomo* (#28, no. 1).

池田さんは風邪で咳が出るのに、タバコばかり吸っています。

Ikeda-san wa kaze de seki ga deru no ni, tabako bakari sutte imasu.

Even though Ikeda is coughing from a cold, all he does is smoke cigarettes [he is (still) smoking all the time].

山本さんのパーティーには行かないと言ったのに、どうして行くんですか。

Yamamoto-san no pātī ni wa ikanai to itta no ni, dō shite iku-n desu ka.

You said you wouldn't go to Yamamoto's party, so why are you going? / Why are you going to Yamamoto's party when you said you wouldn't?

*2. Used at the end of a sentence, indicates a feeling of dissatisfaction: ''despite the fact that, even though.''

Note: This usage is essentially the same as no. 1, above, except that the second clause isn't stated outright. (Words in brackets below show only one of various imaginable contexts.)

勉強をしなさいと言ったのに……

Benkyō o shinasai to itta no ni . . .

Despite the fact that I told you to study [you didn't, and are now in hot water]. / I *told* you to study!

交通事故を起こさないように気をつけていたのに……

Kōtsū-jiko o okosanai yō ni ki o tsukete ita no ni . . .

Even though I tried to be careful so as not to have an accident . . . [I smashed up the car anyway]. / I *was* trying my best not to get involved in a automobile accident.

3. ''To, in order to.''

ここから湖へ行くのに何時間ぐらいかかりますか。

Koko kara mizuumi e iku no ni nanjikan gurai kakarimasu ka.

How long does it take to get from here to the lake? (Lit., In order to get from here to the lake, about how many hours will it take?)

漢字を覚えるのにいい方法を教えて下さい。

Kanji o oboeru no ni ii hōhō o oshiete kudasai.

Please tell me a good way to learn *kanji*.

31 — KUSE NI | くせに

1. ''Despite the fact that, though.''

Note: This usage is similar to that of *no ni* (#30, no. 1), but there is an added feeling of censure or contempt.

子供のくせに、大人の話に口を出してはいけません。

Kodomo no kuse ni, otona no hanashi ni kuchi o dashite wa ikemasen.

Children shouldn't interrupt when grown-ups are talking. (Lit., Despite the fact [or considering the fact] you are a [mere] child, you are not to butt in on grown-up's talk [the way you are doing].)

あの人は能力もないくせに、地位だけは欲しがっている。

Ano hito wa nōryoku mo nai kuse ni, chii dake wa hoshigatte iru.

Despite the fact that he has no ability, all he wants is status.

2. Used at the end of a sentence to express censure or contempt.

あなただってできないくせに……

Anata datte dekinai kuse ni . . .

As if you could do it yourself. (Lit., Despite the fact that even you couldn't do it [you are trying to tell me how to].)

自分でもわからないくせに……

Jibun de mo wakaranai kuse ni . . .

As if *you* understood. (Lit., Despite the fact that even you don't understand [you presume to give advice to others].)

32 — MONO NO ものの

*1. "But, although."

Note: *Mono no* means essentially the same thing as *ga* (#2, II) and *keredomo* (#28), but is a more formal usage and is used more often in writing than speaking.

その国は独立したものの、まだ経済的な問題がたくさんある。

*Sono kuni wa dokuritsu shita **mono no**, mada keizai-teki na mondai ga takusan aru.*

Although the country has become independent, it still has many economic problems.

アメリカへ留学することに決めたものの、奨学金を取るのがむずかしい。

*Amerika e ryūgaku suru koto ni kimeta **mono no**, shōgaku-kin o toru no ga muzukashii.*

Although I've decided to study in the United States, it's difficult to get a scholarship.

33 — | TOKORO GA | ところが

Note: *Tokoro ga* is always used after the *-ta* form of a verb. The tense of this verb, however, is not necessarily past, but is determined by the tense of the verb in the main clause.

1. Used between two clauses to indicate that they are opposed in meaning; the result is often unexpected (a. bad result; b. good result): "but, although, when."

a) Indicating a bad result.

銀行へ行ったところが、もう閉まっていた。

*Ginkō e itta **tokoro ga**, mō shimatte ita.*

I went to the bank, but it was already closed. / When I got to the bank, it was already closed.

あの人に会いに行ったところが、会議中で会えなかった。

*Ano hito ni ai ni itta **tokoro ga**, kaigi-chū de aenakatta.*

I went to see her, but I couldn't because she was in a meeting.

b) Indicating a good result.

K大学には合格できないと思っていたところが、合格通知が来た。

*K daigaku ni wa gōkaku dekinai to omotte ita **tokoro ga**, gōkaku tsūchi ga kita.*

Although I thought I wouldn't pass [the entrance exam to] K University, I received a notice that I had.

あまり期待していなかった**ところが**、そのコンサートはすばらしかった。

*Amari kitai shite inakatta **tokoro ga**, sono konsāto wa subarashikatta.*

Although I hadn't really been expecting much, the concert was fabulous.

34 — -BA | ば

1. Indicates a supposition and result: "if . . . then."

Note: *-Tara* (#35, no. 1) is similar in usage.

明日天気がよければ、ドライブに行きましょう。

Ashita tenki ga yokereba, doraibu ni ikimashō.

If the weather is nice tomorrow, let's go for a drive.

お金があれば、大きい家が買いたいですね。

Okane ga areba, ōkii ie ga kaitai desu ne.

If I had the money, I'd like to buy a big house.

2. Indicates that the clause after *-ba* is the result of the clause before it: "if . . . then."

Note: *To* (#6, III-3) can also be used here.

六甲山に登れば、神戸の街がきれいに見えますよ。

Rokkō-san ni noboreba, Kōbe no machi ga kirei ni miemasu yo.

If you climb Mt. Rokko, you can get a good view of the city of Kobe.

よく練習すれば、このピアノ曲が弾けるようになります。

Yoku renshū sureba, kono piano-kyoku ga hikeru yō ni narimasu.

If you practice hard, you'll be able to play this piano piece.

*3. Used to introduce a clause: "if" (but not a cause-effect relationship).

よろしければ、お菓子を召し上がって下さい。

Yoroshikereba, okashi o meshiagatte kudasai.

If you would like, please have some of the sweets.

考えてみれば、よくこんなに会社が大きくなったものだ。

Kangaete mireba, yoku konna ni kaisha ga ōkiku natta mono da.

If you think about it, it is remarkable that the company has gotten this big.

4. Idiomatic usages of the -*ba* conditional.

a) . . . *ieba*: ". . . stated."

簡単に言えば、それは無理だということでしょう。

Kantan ni ieba, sore wa muri da to iu koto deshō.

Simply stated, that means it is impossible. (Lit., If we state it simply . . .)

b) *Dekireba*: "if possible (lit., if it can be done)."

できれば明後日の方が私は都合がいいんですが……

Dekireba myōgonichi no hō ga watashi wa tsugō ga ii-n desu ga . . .

If possible, the day after tomorrow would be better for me.

*5. Used to connect two similar events or states: "and."

今日は、天気もよければ風もないで、お花見には最適です。

Kyō wa, tenki mo yokereba kaze mo nai de, ohanami ni wa saiteki desu.

Today is perfect for flower-viewing: the weather is nice and there's no wind.

戦後は米もなければ野菜もないで、たいへんでしたよ。

Sengo wa kome mo nakereba yasai mo nai de, taihen deshita yo.

After the war there was no rice and there were no vegetables; [things] were very difficult.

6. In the form V-*ba ii*: "one ought to do, one need only do."

本を借りるには、ここに名前を書けばいいんです。

Hon o kariru ni wa, koko ni namae o kakeba ii-n desu.

To borrow a book, you need only write your name here.

たしかに宿題を忘れたのは君の責任ですが、先生にあやまりさえすればいいんです。

Tashika ni shukudai o wasureta no wa kimi no sekinin desu ga, sensei ni ayamari sae sureba ii-n desu.

While it was certainly your fault that you forgot the homework, all you have to do is apologize to the teacher.

35 — | -TARA | たら |

1. Indicates a supposition and result: "if . . . then."

Note: This usage is similar to *-ba* (#34, no. 1), although *-tara* sounds somewhat more gentle. *-Tara* is likely to be used when the result is an intention, request (command), or question.

その料理があまり辛かったら、私は食べないわ。

Sono ryōri ga amari karakattara, watashi wa tabenai wa.

If that dish is too spicy, I won't eat it.

彼に会ったら、よろしくと言って下さい。

Kare ni attara, yoroshiku to itte kudasai.

If you see him, give him my regards (say hello).

山田さんの都合が悪かったら、誰にワープロをたのみましょうか。

Yamada-san no tsugō ga warukattara, dare ni wāpuro o tanomimashō ka.

If Yamada is busy (unavailable, occupied, is otherwise engaged), who shall we ask to do the word-processing?

2. Used at the end of a sentence to indicate a proposal; used often by women: "how about, why not."

もう遅いから、その仕事明日になさったら。

Mō osoi kara, sono shigoto ashita ni nasattara.

It's late, so why not do that work tomorrow.

それは小さいから、こちらの大きいのをお買いになったら。

Sore wa chiisai kara, kochira no ōkii no o okai ni nattara.

That one is small, so why not buy this big one [instead].

3. Used at the end of a sentence to indicate irritation or impatience, with a meaning something like "I tell you, I'm telling you."

Note: Whereas with the above usages *-tara* is added to a verb stem in the same way as the past-tense ending *-ta*, in this usage *-ttara* is added to the *-te* and *-nasai* form of verbs.

早くしてったら……

Hayaku shite-ttara . . .

C'mon, get a move on!

もう寝なさいったら……

Mō nenasai-ttara.

Get to bed, I say [I'm telling you]!

4. Indicates an action which is followed by something being learned: "when."

Note: *To* (#6, III-4) is similar to *-tara* in this usage.

友達の家へ行ったら、彼は留守だった。

Tomodachi no ie e ittara, kare wa rusu datta.

When I went to my friend's house, [I found that] he was out. / I went to my friend's home, but he was out.

ホテルに電話をしたら、部屋はいっぱいだった。

Hoteru ni denwa o shitara, heya wa ippai datta.

When I called the hotel, [I found that] all the rooms were full. / I called the hotel, but all the rooms were taken.

5. Indicates that one action follows immediately upon another: "when, as soon as."

私が声をかけたら来て下さい。

Watashi ga koe o kaketara kite kudasai.

Please come [right away] when I call you.

この仕事が終ったら、そちらへ行きます。

Kono shigoto ga owattara, sochira e ikimasu.

I'll be there as soon as this work is done [as soon as I'm finished here].

36 — | NARA | なら

Note: See also *mono nara* (#37).

1. Indicates a supposition and result: "if . . . then."

Note: *Nara* is often used after nouns. It is similar to *-ba* (#34, no. 1), *-tara* (#35, no. 1), and *to* (#6, III-3).

私は午後なら暇がありますよ。

Watashi wa gogo nara hima ga arimasu yo.

If [it's in] the afternoon, I'm free. / I'll be free in the afternoon.

明日雨なら、ゴルフに行かないつもりです。

Ashita ame nara, gorufu ni ikanai tsumori desu.

Tomorrow, if it's raining, I don't intend to go golfing. / I don't plan to go golfing tomorrow if it rains.

あの人が行くなら、私は行きたくないですね。

Ano hito ga iku nara, watashi wa ikitaku nai desu ne.

If she's going, I sure don't want to.

Note: A major difference between *nara* and *-tara* is that the clause after *nara* emphasizes what would (definitely) take place if the supposed event were to occur, whereas the result clause after *-tara* emphasizes what would "happen to" take place.

乗るなら飲むな。飲んだら乗るな。

Noru nara nomu na. Nondara noru na.

If you [are going to] drive, don't drink. If you have drunk, don't drive.

2. Indicates that a topic is being brought up: "as for."

その問題なら、もう解決しました。

Sono mondai nara, mō kaiketsu shimashita.

As for that problem, it has already been settled.

和歌の参考書なら、佐々木先生の研究室にある。

Waka no sankō-sho nara, Sasaki-sensei no kenkyū-shitsu ni aru.

If it's reference books on *waka* [that you're looking for], they're in Professor Sasaki's office.

37 — MONO NARA | ものなら

*1. After a potential verb or *-ō/-yō* form of a verb, indicates a condition and result, with an added sense of censure or threat: "if . . . then."

あなたにできるものなら、やってみて下さい。

Anata ni dekiru mono nara, yatte mite kudasai.

If it's something you can do, go ahead and do it. / If you think you can do it, go ahead and try.

政治家がそんなばかなことをしようものなら、国民は黙っていませんよ。

Seiji-ka ga sonna baka na koto o shiyō mono nara, kokumin wa damatte imasen yo.

If the politicians do something stupid like that, the people aren't going to keep quiet about it.

*2. Indicates a condition and bad result: "if . . . then."

課長がそんなやり方をしようものなら、部下は課長を全然信頼しなくなるでしょうね。

Kachō ga sonna yarikata o shiyō mono nara, buka wa kachō o zenzen shinrai shinaku naru deshō ne.

If the section chief goes about it in that way, his subordinates will lose all faith in him.

これ以上仕事を続けよう**ものなら**、あなたは死んでしまいますよ。

Kore ijō shigoto o tsuzukeyō mono nara, anata wa shinde shimaimasu yo.

If you work any more [any harder] than this, you're going to die, you know. / If you continue working the way you are now, you will end up killing yourself.

*3. Expresses a fancied hope or desire: "if . . . then."

空を飛べる**ものなら**飛んでみたい。

Sora o toberu mono nara tonde mitai.

If it were possible to fly [in the sky], I would like to try it.

会社へ行かなくていい**ものなら**行きたくない。

Kaisha e ikanakute ii mono nara ikitaku nai.

If it were all right not to go to work, I wouldn't [want to] go. / I wouldn't go to work if I didn't have to.

38 — TOKORO | ところ

1. Indicates that one is on the verge of doing something; preceded by the root form of the verb: "just about to."

これから出かける**ところ**なので、ゆっくり話をする時間はありません。

Kore kara dekakeru tokoro na no de, yukkuri hanashi o suru jikan wa arimasen.

Since I'm just about to go out, I don't have time for a leisurely talk.

山田さんに電話をする**ところ**ですが、何か伝言はありませんか。

*Yamada-san ni denwa o suru **tokoro** desu ga, nani ka dengon wa arimasen ka.*

I'm just about to call Yamada. Do you have any messages for him?

2. Indicates that an action is presently taking place (preceded by V-*te iru*).

今手紙を書いているところです。

*Ima tegami o kaite iru **tokoro** desu.*

I am writing a letter just now. / I am in the midst of writing a letter.

役員は、今その問題を検討しているところです。

*Yakuin wa, ima sono mondai o kentō shite iru **tokoro** desu.*

The directors now have that problem under advisement. / The directors are just now taking that problem under consideration.

3. Indicates that an action has just come to an end (preceded by V-*ta*).

彼は今成田に着いたところです。

*Kare wa ima Narita ni tsuita **tokoro** desu.*

He just now arrived at Narita [Airport].

広田さんは、今日フランスから帰国したところですよ。

*Hirota-san wa, kyō Furansu kara kikoku shita **tokoro** desu yo.*

Hirota just today returned from France.

4. Indicates the conclusion of a certain action at the end of a clause: "when, upon."

Note: This usage (in contrast to V-*tara . . . datta*) has a somewhat stiff sound, and is thus more often found in writing.

デパートに問い合わせてみたところ、その品物は売り切れだった。

*Depāto ni toiawasete mita **tokoro**, sono shinamono wa uri-kire datta.*

When I inquired at the department store, [I found that] the item was sold out. (Or, Upon asking at the department store, ...)

大学の図書館で調べた**ところ**、その作家は詩も書いていたことがわかった。

*Daigaku no tosho-kan de shirabeta **tokoro**, sono sakka wa shi mo kaite ita koto ga wakatta.*

When I checked at the university library, I learned that the writer had written poems as well. (Or, Upon checking at the university library, ...)

39 — | MONO O | ものを

*1. Usually used at the end of a sentence, indicating resentment or complaint.

お知らせ下されば、病院へお見舞いに参りました**もの を**……

*Oshirase kudasareba, byōin e omimai ni mairimashita **mono o** ...*

If only you had told me, I would have come to see you at the hospital.

私にできることでしたら、お手伝いしました**ものを**……

*Watashi ni dekiru koto deshitara, otetsudai shimashita **mono o** ...*

If there had been something I could have done, I would have helped out.

40 — | -NAGARA | ながら

1. Indicates that two actions are taking place simultaneously: ''as, while.''

Note: The subject of both clauses must be the same. In English translation, the main and subordinate clauses of the Japanese are usually reversed.

毎朝テレビを見**ながら**、朝ご飯を食べます。

*Maiasa terebi o mi**nagara**, asagohan o tabemasu.*

Every morning, I watch television as I eat breakfast. (Lit., . . . I eat breakfast as I watch television.)

青木さんはいつも音楽を聞き**ながら**勉強している。

*Aoki-san wa itsu mo ongaku o kiki**nagara** benkyō shite iru.*

Aoki always listens to music while he studies. (Lit., Aoki studies while he listens to music.)

2. Used between two clauses to emphasize that they are opposed in meaning: "although, while."

高木さんは体が弱いと言い**ながら**、よく夜遅くまで酒を飲んでいる。

*Takagi-san wa karada ga yowai to ii**nagara**, yoku yoru osoku made sake o nonde iru.*

Although Takagi says he has a weak constitution [poor health], he often drinks until late at night.

あの先生は学生には遅刻をしないようにと言い**なが**ら、自分はいつも遅れて学校へ来る。

*Ano sensei wa gakusei ni wa chikoku o shinai yō ni to ii**nagara**, jibun wa itsu mo okurete gakkō e kuru.*

Although that teacher tells her students not to be late, she herself is always late in coming to school.

41 ― -TARI | たり

1. Indicates that several actions are listed in no particular sequence: "such things as."

日曜日はたいてい友達とテニスをし**たり**、映画を見に行っ**たり**します。

*Nichiyōbi wa taitei tomodachi to tenisu o shi**tari**, eiga o mi ni ittari shimasu.*

On Sundays I usually do such things as play tennis with my friends or go to see movies.

旅行中は美術館に行ったりお土産を買ったりで、あっ
という間に時間がなくなりました。

Ryokō-chū wa bijutsu-kan ni ittari omiyage o kattari de, atto iu ma ni jikan ga nakunarimashita.

Time passed quickly during the trip, what with going to museums, buying souvenirs for people back home, and such.

Note: Used with only one verb, *-tari* indicates that the action of the verb is representative of a number of actions: "such things as . . ."

天気の悪い日には、家で音楽を聞いたりします。

Tenki no warui hi ni wa, ie de ongaku o kiitari shimasu.

On days when the weather is bad, I listen to music and do other such things at home.

2. Indicates that several like actions are performed.

午前中は漢字を書いたり読んだりする。

Gozen-chū wa kanji o kaitari yondari suru.

In the morning I read and write *kanji*.

この頃その俳優のことをテレビや雑誌で聞いたり見た
りします。

Konogoro sono haiyū no koto o terebi ya zasshi de kiitari mitari shimasu.

These days we [often] see and hear about that actor on TV and in the magazines.

3. Indicates repetition of contrasting actions.

そんなにテレビをつけたり消したりしないでちょうだ
い。

Sonna ni terebi o tsuketari keshitari shinaide chōdai.

Stop turning the TV on and off like that.

今週、株は上がったり下がったりしています。

Konshū, kabu wa agattari sagattari shite imasu.

Stocks are going up and down this week.

4. Used with the same verb in positive and negative forms: "sometimes I do and sometimes I don't."

父は体の調子によって、ゴルフに行ったり行かなかったりします。

Chichi wa karada no chōshi ni yotte, gorufu ni ittari ikanakattari shimasu.

My father goes to play golf [and not to play golf] depending on his physical condition.

日曜日には、テレビを見たり見なかったりします。

Nichiyōbi ni wa, terebi o mitari minakattari shimasu.

Sometimes I watch TV on Sundays and sometimes I don't.

42 — | SHI | し |

1. Indicates (and often emphasizes) the occurrence or existence of two or more actions or states: "and, as well as."

ハワイは気候はいいし、花も美しいし、いいところですよ。

Hawai wa kikō wa ii shi, hana mo utsukushii shi, ii tokoro desu yo.

Hawaii is a nice place: the climate is good, and the flowers are beautiful.

新しい課長は頑固だし、仕事もできないですよ。

Atarashii kachō wa ganko da shi, shigoto mo dekinai desu yo.

The new section chief is pigheaded and can't do the work either.

2. Indicates a reason or reasons for the following conclusion: "and . . . , so."

竹村さんは、みんなから信頼されていないし、人気もないし、グループをまとめるのは無理でしょう。

Takemura-san wa, minna kara shinrai sarete inai shi, ninki mo nai shi, gurūpu o matomeru no wa muri deshō.

Takemura is not trusted by anyone and is not popular, so it would be impossible for him to lead the group.

あのレストランは、サービスは悪いし、料理はまずい
し、行かない方がいいですよ。

*Ano resutoran wa, sābisu wa warui shi, ryōri wa mazui shi,
ikanai hō ga ii desu yo.*

The service at that restaurant is bad and the food is poor, so
you had better not go there.

43 — TOMO｜とも

1. Used after numbers and counters: "both, all (three,
etc.)."

ここにいる人たちは、3人とも大学で言語学を勉強し
ました。

*Koko ni iru hitotachi wa, sannin tomo daigaku de gengo-gaku
o benkyō shimashita.*

All three of the people here studied linguistics in college. (Lit.,
As for the people who are here, all three . . .)

このセーターは、2枚ともMサイズですか。

Kono sētā wa, nimai tomo M-saizu desu ka.

Are both of these sweaters mediums?

2. After the *-ku* form of adjectives, indicates an approximate maximum or minimum: "at the least, most,
latest, etc."

この家なら、少なくとも1億円はするでしょう。

Kono ie nara, sukunaku tomo ichioku-en wa suru deshō.

This house would cost at least 100 million yen.

この事故で死んだ人は、多くとも100人ぐらいだろう。

Kono jiko de shinda hito wa, ōku tomo hyakunin gurai darō.

The [number of] fatalities in this accident was 100 people at
most.

3. Indicates inclusion: "including."

サービス料とも合計 1 万5000円です。

*Sābisu-ryō **tomo** gōkei ichiman-gosen-en desu.*

The total is ¥15,000, including the service charge.

運賃ともで、 5 万円になりますが。

*Unchin **tomo** de, goman-en ni narimasu ga.*

It comes to ¥50,000, including freight.

*4. Used after the -ō form of a verb, adds emphasis to a supposition: "even if, no matter."

あの人ならどんな事があろうとも、最後まで頑張るだろう。

*Ano hito nara donna koto ga arō **tomo**, saigo made ganbaru darō.*

No matter what happens, he [if anyone] will stick it out to the bitter end.

明日は雪が降ろうとも、行くつもりだ。

*Ashita wa yuki ga furō **tomo**, iku tsumori da.*

Even if it should snow tomorrow, I intend to go.

*5. In the form *tomo arō* (noun) *ga*: "of all people (things)."

首相ともあろう人が、そんなことをして平気だとは信じられない。

*Shushō **tomo** arō hito ga, sonna koto o shite heiki da to wa shinjirarenai.*

For the prime minister, of all people, to do something like that and be calm [about it] is unbelievable. / I can't believe that someone in the position of prime minister could do something like that without the slightest qualm.

大学の学長ともあろう人が、あんなにビジョンがないのでは困る。

*Daigaku no gakuchō **tomo** arō hito ga, anna ni bijon ga nai no de wa komaru.*

For the president of the university, of all people, to be so lacking in vision is a problem (troublesome). / We're in trouble (in a fix, in bad shape) if the person who is supposed to be the president of the university is so lacking in vision.

6. Appearing after two words of opposite meaning and followed by *ienai*: "can't say (yes) or (no)."

多田さんは、あの映画はいい**とも**悪い**とも**言えないと言ってました。

*Tada-san wa, ano eiga wa ii **tomo** warui **tomo** ienai to itte mashita.*

Tada said that he couldn't say whether the movie was good or bad. / Tada said that it was hard to say whether the movie was good or bad.

その値段は、高い**とも**安い**とも**言えませんね。

*Sono nedan wa, takai **tomo** yasui **tomo** iemasen ne.*

It's hard to say whether the price is high or low.

7. At the end of a sentence, adds decisiveness to a positive statement: "indeed, certainly, of course."

この本を借りていいですか。
いい**とも**。

Kono hon o karite ii desu ka.
*Ii **tomo**.*

May I borrow this book?
Certainly.

明日の試合に行きますか。
行く**とも**。

Ashita no shiai ni ikimasu ka.
*Iku **tomo**.*

Are you going to the game tomorrow?
I certainly am.

44 — | YARA | やら

1. Joins nouns to indicate a non-exhaustive list of items: "such things as . . . ; and, what with."

Note: This usage is essentially the same as *ya*, *to ka*, and *dano*, although these three are used more often in the spoken language.

あの国の人たちは、戦争やら、インフレやらで大変で しょうね。

Ano kuni no hitotachi wa, sensō yara, infure yara de taihen deshō ne.

What with war, inflation, and the like, the people of that country must be having a hard time.

その大学には、イギリス人やらフランス人やら、いろ いろな国の人がいますよ。

Sono daigaku ni wa, Igirisu-jin yara Furansu-jin yara, iroiro na kuni no hito ga imasu yo.

At that university there are people from various countries, such as England and France. (Lit., . . . such as Englishmen and Frenchmen.)

2. Used with words of opposite meaning, or with positive and negative forms of the same word. *Ka* can replace *yara* in this usage, but the latter is softer in tone: "whether, whether or not."

久美ちゃんはこのお菓子が好きなのやら、嫌いなのや ら何も言わないんです。

Kumi-chan wa kono okashi ga suki na no yara, kirai na no yara nani mo iwanai-n desu.

Kumi doesn't say anything about whether she likes or dislikes this candy. / Kumi won't say whether she likes the candy or not.

パーティーに行くのやら行かないのやら、はっきりし て下さい。

Pātī ni iku no yara ikanai no yara, hakkiri shite kudasai.

Please make it clear [say, make up your mind, decide] whether or not you are going to the party.

3. Used with interrogative words, expresses uncertainty (in instances where *wakaranai* is not explicit, it is understood).

Note: This usage is similar to, but a little softer than, *ka* (#11, II-3).

あの犬はどこへ行った**のやら**、わからないんですよ。

Ano inu wa doko e itta no yara, wakaranai-n desu yo.

I have no idea where that dog went.

研くんはどの大学に入れる**やら**、本当に心配です。

Ken-kun wa dono daigaku ni haireru yara, hontō ni shinpai desu.

I'm really worried about which university Ken will be able to get into.

4. Used at the end of a sentence, indicates a rhetorical question with negative implications: "I wonder."

来年はどんな年になる**やら**……

Rainen wa donna toshi ni naru yara . . .

I wonder what kind of year next year will be. / I wonder how next year will turn out.

日本の将来はどうなる**やら**……

Nippon no shōrai wa dō naru yara . . .

I wonder what Japan's future will be like. / I wonder about the future of Japan.

45 — | DANO | だの

1. Indicates a non-exhaustive list of items or actions: "such things as."

Note: *Dano*, a colloquial usage, is similar to *yara* and *to ka*.

クリスマスには、友達から本**だの**、カレンダー**だの**、チョコレート**だの**をもらいました。

Kurisumasu ni wa, tomodachi kara hon dano, karendā dano, chokorēto dano o moraimashita.

At Christmas, I received from friends a book, a calendar, some chocolates, and other such things.

学生のときは、ショパン**だの**リスト**だの**のピアノ曲をよく弾きました。

*Gakusei no toki wa, Shopan **dano** Risuto **dano** no piano-kyoku o yoku hikimashita.*

When I was a student, I played a lot of piano pieces by such composers as Chopin and Liszt.

2. Used for a pair of opposite actions or states (either opposite words or the positive and negative form of the same word).

行くだの行かないだのと言わないで、どちらかに決めて下さい。

*Iku **dano** ikanai **dano** to iwanai de, dochira ka ni kimete kudasai.*

Stop saying that you will go, and then that you won't go; make up your mind one way or the other.

オーストラリアは、今寒いだの、暑いだのと言う人がいて、どちらなのかわかりません。

*Ōsutoraria wa, ima samui **dano**, atsui **dano** to iu hito ga ite, dochira na no ka wakarimasen.*

Since some people say Australia is cold now, and some say it's hot, I'm not sure which it is.

46 — NARI | なり

1. Indicates a choice: "or, whether or not."

Note: This usage is similar to the more common *ka* (#11, II-1), but *nari* lends slightly more emphasis.

その問題について、松田先生なり、高山先生なりに聞いてみて下さい。

*Sono mondai ni tsuite, Matsuda-sensei **nari**, Takayama-sensei **nari** ni kiite mite kudasai.*

Please ask either Professor Matsuda or Professor Takayama about that problem.

明日行くなり、あさって行くなり、早く決めましょう。

*Ashita iku **nari**, asatte iku **nari**, hayaku kimemashō.*

Let's hurry up and decide whether we are going tomorrow or the day after tomorrow. / Are we going tomorrow or the day after tomorrow? Let's hurry up and decide.

2. Indicates a suggestion: "or something."

まだ時間がありますから、喫茶店でお茶を飲むなりしましょうか。

*Mada jikan ga arimasu kara, kissaten de ocha o nomu **nari** shimashō ka.*

Since there's still time, shall we drink some tea at a coffee shop or something?

健康のためにテニスなり、ゴルフなり、何か運動をした方がいいですよ。

Kenkō no tame ni tenisu nari, gorufu nari, nani ka undō o shita hō ga ii desu yo.

For the sake of your health, you had better get some exercise, like playing tennis or golf.

*3. Indicates that a second action follows immediately upon the action preceding it: "as soon as."

Note: This usage is similar to *to* (#6, III-1) and *-tara* (#35, no. 5).

信号が青になるなり、待っていた車が走り出した。

*Shingō ga ao ni naru **nari**, matte ita kuruma ga hashiridashita.*

As soon as the light turned green, the waiting cars began moving.

山本さんが電車に飛び乗るなり、ドアが閉まった。

*Yamamoto-san ga densha ni tobinoru **nari**, doa ga shimatta.*

As soon as Yamamoto jumped into the train, the doors closed.

*4. The expression *nan nari*: "whatever, anything."

ご不満なことがあったら、何なりとおっしゃって下さい。

*Go-fuman na koto ga attara, nan **nari** to osshatte kudasai.*

If there is anything unsatisfactory, please say so [lit., say whatever it is].

**5. The expression *dai nari shō nari*: "whether big or small."

どこにでも、大なり小なり問題はあるでしょう。

*Doko ni de mo, dai **nari** shō **nari** mondai wa aru deshō.*

There are problems everywhere—some big, some small. / Everyone has problems, whether they be big or small.

---

47 —
-TE WA (-DE WA)
ては（では）

Note: Here we are concerned with *wa* in combination with the *-te* (*-de*) form of verbs. See also *wa* (#1, particularly no. 5) and *to wa* (#17).

1. Indicates the repetition of two contrasting, alternating actions.

デビッドさんは、漢字を書いては消し、書いては消ししています。

*Debiddo-san wa, kanji o kaite **wa** keshi, kaite **wa** keshi shite imasu.*

David writes the *kanji* and erases them, and writes and erases them [again].

海岸には波が、寄せては返し、返しては寄せています。

*Kaigan ni wa nami ga, yosete **wa** kaeshi, kaeshite **wa** yosete imasu.*

At the shore, the waves advance and recede, recede and advance.

2. In the form *ni shite wa* (or *to shite wa*): "for."

日曜日にしては、デパートがすいていますね。

Nichiyōbi ni shite wa, depāto ga suite imasu ne.

For a Sunday, the department stores are not very crowded.

あの人は日本人にしては、英語がうまいですね。

Ano hito wa Nihon-jin ni shite wa, Eigo ga umai desu ne.

For a Japanese, her English is pretty good.

3. A conditional pattern, always with the result clause in the negative or with a negative implication.

a) Indicates an undesirable possibility leading to a negative result.

「腹が減っては戦ができぬ」と昔の人は言いました。

"Hara ga hette wa ikusa ga dekinu" to mukashi no hito wa iimashita.

"You can't fight on an empty stomach," people said of old.

b) In the form *-te wa komaru*: "there will be problems if; you shouldn't."

ここに車を止めては困ります。

Koko ni kuruma o tomete wa komarimasu.

You shouldn't park the car here. (Lit, Parking the car here will be inconvenient [troublesome, a bother].)

c) In the forms *-te wa ikenai* or *-te wa naranai*: "you shouldn't, you mustn't."

公園で花を取ってはいけません。

Kōen de hana o totte wa ikemasen.

You should not pick flowers in the park.

ここでタバコを吸ってはならない。

Koko de tabako o sutte wa naranai.

You must not smoke here.

d) In the form *-te wa irarenai*: "be unable to."

この問題については、私は黙ってはいられません。

Kono mondai ni tsuite wa, watashi wa damatte wa iraremasen.

I cannot remain silent about this problem.

48 — | DOKORO | どころ |

1. Emphasizes a negative action or state as against the impossibility of a contrasting positive action or state: "it is out of the question, unthinkable, far from."

この頃は仕事が忙しくて、旅行に行くどころではない。

*Konogoro wa shigoto ga isogashikute, ryokō ni iku **dokoro** de wa nai.*

I've been so busy lately, taking a trip is unthinkable.

あの人は秀才どころの話じゃなくて、まるで天才ですね。

*Ano hito wa shūsai **dokoro** no hanashi ja nakute, maru de tensai desu ne.*

It is not a matter of his being brilliant; he is an absolute genius.

2. In the form *dokoro ka*, negates the first of two parallel nouns: "far from; not merely."

普通は１時間ぐらいかかるが、昨日は道が混んでいて、１時間どころか３時間もかかった。

*Futsū wa ichi-jikan gurai kakaru ga, kinō wa michi ga konde ite, ichi-jikan **dokoro** ka san-jikan mo kakatta.*

Ordinarily it takes an hour, but yesterday the roads were so crowded that, far from one hour, it took three.

あの人は英語どころか、フランス語もよくできますよ。

*Ano hito wa Eigo **dokoro** ka, Furansu-go mo yoku dekimasu yo.*

He is good not merely at English, but at French as well.

49 — | TOSHITE | として |

1. Indicates status or position: "in the capacity of, as."

ショパンは、ポーランドの作曲家として有名です。

*Shopan wa, Pōrando no sakkyoku-ka **toshite** yūmei desu.*

Chopin is famous as a Polish composer.

こちらが、交換学生として日本へ来たホワイトさんです。

*Kochira ga, kōkan-gakusei **toshite** Nihon e kita Howaito-san desu.*

This is Ms. White, who has come to Japan as an exchange student.

*2. Used with "one" and counters incorporating "one": "without exception."

あの人たちのする仕事は、1つとしていいものがないんです。

*Ano hitotachi no suru shigoto wa, hitotsu **toshite** ii mono ga nai-n desu.*

You can't say one good thing about the work they do. (Lit., [Of] the work those people do, there is not one good thing.)

課長はマージャンに、1度として勝ったことがありません。

*Kachō wa mājan ni, ichido **toshite** katta koto ga arimasen.*

The section chief has never once won at Majong.

50 — | YORI | より

Note: *Yori* is sometimes displaced by nonstandard *yori mo* and *yori ka*.

1. Indicates a comparison: "than."

吉田さんは小出さんより背が高いです。

*Yoshida-san wa Koide-san **yori** se ga takai desu.*

Yoshida is taller than Koide.

ニューヨークより東京の方が、人口が多いです。

Nyūyōku yori Tōkyō no hō ga, jinkō ga ōi desu.

The population of Tokyo is greater than that of New York.

*2. In the form *to iu yori*: "rather."

あの人は指導者というより、独裁者です。

Ano hito wa shidō-sha to iu yori, dokusai-sha desu.

He is a dictator rather than a leader. / He is more of a dictator than a leader.

A大学の学長は、学者というより政治家だ。

A daigaku no gakuchō wa, gakusha to iu yori seiji-ka da.

The president of A University is more of a politician than a scholar.

*3. Used with interrogative words, indicates that the thing previously mentioned is in the superlative.

この店のフランス料理は、どこよりおいしいと思います。

Kono mise no Furansu-ryōri wa, doko yori oishii to omoi-masu.

I think that the French food at this restaurant is better than anywhere else.

彼は私にプロポーズしたとき、「僕は誰よりも君を愛している」と言ったのよ。

Kare wa watashi ni puropōzu shita toki, "boku wa dare yori mo kimi o aishite iru" to itta no yo.

When he proposed to me, he said, "I love you more than anyone."

お元気そうで何よりです。

Ogenki-sō de nani yori desu.

I'm glad to see you looking so well. (Lit., Your looking well is more than anything.)

*4. Indicates the time or place at which at an action begins: "from, at."

Note: This usage is equivalent to *kara* (#15, I-1 [time] and I-2 [place]), although *yori* is more formal and is more commonly used in writing and elevated speech.

3時より閣議が行われます。

Sanji yori kakugi ga okonawaremasu.

A cabinet meeting will begin at [be held from] three o'clock.

この国境より向こうが中国です。

Kono kokkyō yori mukō ga Chūgoku desu.

From this [point of the] border on is China. / On the other side of this border is China.

*5. Indicates a place or position from which an action occurs: "from."

電車がまいりますから、白線より後ろに下がってお待ちください。

Densha ga mairimasu kara, hakusen yori ushiro ni sagatte omachi kudasai.

A train is coming, so please step back from the white line and wait. / A train is arriving. Please wait behind the white line.

私の家は駅より手前にある。

Watashi no ie wa eki yori temae ni aru.

My house is on this side of the station. (Lit., My house is before where the station is.)

*6. Indicates a cause, reason, or motivation: "as a result of."

先月の市場調査より次のような結果が明らかになった。

Sengetsu no shijō-chōsa yori tsugi no yō na kekka ga akiraka ni natta.

As a result of last month's market research, the following results have come to light.

河川の汚染より伝染病が発生した。

Kasen no osen yori densen-byō ga hassei shita.

Infectious diseases have broken out as a result of [due to] polluted rivers.

*7. In the form *yori hoka nai*, indicates a limiting of choices to one only: "there is nothing else but."

ここまでやったんですから、終わりまでやる**より**ほか
ないでしょう。

*Koko made yatta-n desu kara, owari made yaru **yori** hoka nai
deshō.*

Since we've done this much, there is nothing else to do but
finish it. / Since we've come this far, we'll just have to finish
it.

停電だから、電気がつくまで待っている**より**ほかな
い。

*Teiden da kara, denki ga tsuku made matte iru **yori** hoka nai.*

Because it's a power failure, there is nothing else to do but
wait till the electricity comes on. / Since there's been a power
outage, we'll simply have to wait until the electricity comes
on.

51 — | SAE | さえ

1. "Even."

Note: This usage is similar to *de mo* (#5, no. 2), but is more emphatic.

その問題は先生で**さえ**答えられなかった。

*Sono mondai wa sensei de **sae** kotaerarenakatta.*

Even the teacher couldn't answer that [test] question.

そんな簡単なことは、子供で**さえ**知っていますよ。

*Sonna kantan na koto wa, kodomo de **sae** shitte imasu yo.*

Even a child knows such a simple thing! / A mere child would
know something as simple as that.

2. In the form *sae . . . -tara* or *sae . . . -ba*, implies that
if something additional is (had been) done, a positive
outcome will occur (would have occurred): "if only."

もう５分**さえ**あったら、飛行機に間に合ったのに……

*Mō gofun **sae** attara, hikō-ki ni ma-ni-atta no ni . . .*

If we had had only five more minutes, we would have been on
time for the flight.

健ちゃんは頭がいいんですから、勉強さえすればいい
大学に入れますよ。

*Ken-chan wa atama ga ii-n desu kara, benkyō sae sureba ii
daigaku ni hairemasu yo.*

Ken has a good head on his shoulders, so if he only studies,
he'll be able to get into a good university.

52 — SURA | すら

*1. "Even."

Note: This more formal equivalent of *sae* (#51, no. 1) is seen most
often in negative sentences.

山田さんは英語の教師なのに、日常会話すらできな
い。

*Yamada-san wa Eigo no kyōshi na no ni, nichijō-kaiwa sura
dekinai.*

Although Yamada is an English teacher, she can't even carry
on an ordinary conversation.

山で救助された人たちは、疲労で動くことすらできな
かった。

*Yama de kyūjo sareta hitotachi wa, hirō de ugoku koto sura
dekinakatta.*

The people rescued in the mountains were so exhausted they
couldn't even move.

53 — KOSO | こそ

1. Adds emphasis to the word preceding it.

来年こそ、ヨーロッパへ旅行したいと思っています。

Rainen koso, Yōroppa e ryokō shitai to omotte imasu.

Next year for certain, I am thinking of making a trip to
Europe. / Next year for sure, I hope to make a trip to Europe.

今度こそ、頑張りましょう。

Kondo koso, ganbarimashō.

Let's give it our best this time.

2. In the idiomatic expression *kochira koso*: "not at all, the pleasure is all mine."

どうも有難うございました。
こちらこそ。

Dōmo arigatō gozaimashita.
Kochira koso.

Thank you very much.
The pleasure is all mine. (Lit., It is precisely me [who should be thanking you].)

Sentence-ending Particles

There are many sentence-ending particles in Japanese. Used commonly in the spoken language, these particles, along with the tone of voice in which they are used, help convey emotional nuances, often without actually altering in any way the explicit content of the sentence: e.g., *onegai shimasu*, *onegai shimasu ne*, and *onegai shimasu yo* are all similar in that they express a request, but are softened or emphasized by the appended particle. Furthermore, certain sentence-ending particles are used predominantly by men, others by women. Some particles have both end-of-sentence and mid-sentence usages, such as *ga*, *ka*, *kara*, *made*, *no*, *keredomo*, *no ni*, *kuse ni*, *-tara*, *mono o*, *tomo*, *yara*.

54 — NE | ね

Note: *Ne* is sometimes pronounced *nē*.

1. Indicates emotion or feelings of admiration.

きれいな花ねぇ。

Kirei na hana nē.

What a pretty flower!

すばらしい演奏だったわ**ね**。

*Subarashii ensō datta wa **ne**.*

That was such a wonderful concert.

Note: Here, *wa* indicates that a woman is speaking.

2. Indicates agreement with the other person.

本当にそうです**ね**。

*Hontō ni sō desu **ne**.*

Yes, that's quite true. / That's so true.

おっしゃる通りです**ね**。

*Ossharu tōri desu **ne**.*

Yes, it's just as you say. / You're quite right.

3. Softens a request.

できればぜひお願いします**ね**。

*Dekireba zehi onegai shimasu **ne**.*

If possible, please be sure to [do it]. / If you would [do that], I'd surely appreciate it.

必ず手紙を下さい**ね**。

*Kanarazu tegami o kudasai **ne**.*

Be sure to write [me a letter].

4. Indicates a request for confirmation.

あの本、持って来て下さったでしょう**ね**。

*Ano hon, motte kite kudasatta deshō **ne**.*

You brought me that book, didn't you [as I asked you to]? / I suppose you brought that book for me.

原田さん、今日来ると言ったんです**ね**。

*Harada-san, kyō kuru to itta-n desu **ne**.*

Harada said that he'd be coming today, right? / It was today, wasn't it?, that Harada said he would come.

5. Indicates a mild assertion of, or variance in, opinion.

そうですか**ね**。

Sō desu ka ne.

Oh, is that so? / I wonder. / You think so?

本当にそんなこと起こったんでしょうかね。

Hontō ni sonna koto okotta-n deshō ka ne.

Hmm, I wonder if that's what actually happened [if something like that really happened].

6. Indicates a mild assertion.

あの人たち、何を考えているのかわかりませんね。

Ano hitotachi, nani o kangaete iru no ka wakarimasen ne.

I just can't understand what they're thinking about [what's going on in their minds].

私は北海道の方が寒いと思うんですけどね。

Watashi wa Hokkaidō no hō ga samui to omou-n desu kedo ne.

I would think that Hokkaido is colder.

55 — YO | よ

1. Urges a course of action.

もうだいぶ歩いたから、この辺でちょっと休もうよ。

Mō daibu aruita kara, kono hen de chotto yasumō yo.

Let's take a break about here, guys. We've already walked quite a bit.

あの展覧会へ行ってみましょうよ。

Ano tenran-kai e itte mimashō yo.

Come on, let's go to that exhibition.

2. Indicates a request (somewhat stronger than *ne*, #54, no. 3).

この仕事はあなたしかできませんから、ぜひお願いしますよ。

Kono shigoto wa anata shika dekimasen kara, zehi onegai shimasu yo.

You're the only one who can handle this job, so I really want you to take it on.

私の家にも来て下さいよ。

Watashi no ie ni mo kite kudasai yo.

Come to *my* house, too.

3. Indicates a statement of certainty.

いえ、恵子は小学校を去年出ましたから、もう13歳ですよ。

Ie, Keiko wa shōgakkō o kyonen demashita kara, mō jūsan-sai desu yo.

No, Keiko graduated from elementary school last year, so she's already thirteen years old, you see.

今日は金曜日ですよ。

Kyō wa kin'yōbi desu yo.

Today is Friday, you know. (Stated, for example, after someone has claimed otherwise.)

4. Indicates scolding or contempt.

あの人は仕事ができないわよ。

Ano hito wa shigoto ga dekinai wa yo.

He just can't do the work!

Note: Here, the combination of *wa yo* indicates that a woman is speaking. See #56.

谷さん、そんな悪いことをしてはいけませんよ。

Tani-san, sonna warui koto o shite wa ikemasen yo.

Tani, you shouldn't do anything [bad] like that!

---

56 — | WA | わ |

Note: (1) This *wa* is written with the *kana* わ (or ワ), as opposed to は (or ハ), used for particle #1. (2) *Wa* is used mainly by women.

1. Indicates emotion or feelings of admiration.

今夜のオペラは、本当にすばらしかった**わ**。

Kon'ya no opera wa, hontō ni subarashikatta wa.

The opera tonight was absolutely fabulous.

この生け花は見事です**わ**。

Kono ikebana wa migoto desu wa.

This flower arrangement is simply splendid!

2. Softens the tone of a statement.

ほかの店で買った方がいいと思う**わ**。

Hoka no mise de katta hō ga ii to omou wa.

I think it would be better to buy it at another store. / I think you had better buy it at another store.

私の方が悪かった**わ**。ごめんなさいね。

Watashi no hō ga warukatta wa. Gomen nasai ne.

It was all my fault. I'm so sorry.

57 — KA NA | かな

Note: Used principally by men; the women's equivalent of *ka na* is *kashira* (#58).

1. Indicates uncertainty: "I wonder."

課長、何時に来る**かな**。

Kachō, nanji ni kuru ka na.

What time's the section chief coming, I wonder.

多賀君は、この仕事できる**かな**。

Taga-kun wa, kono shigoto dekiru ka na.

I wonder if Taga can do this job. / Could Taga handle this job? I wonder.

2. Indicates a question to oneself: "I wonder."

今日は何曜日だった**かな**。

Kyō wa nan-yōbi datta ka na.

Hmm, what day is today?

田中さんと会うのは何時だった**かな**。

Tanaka-san to au no wa nanji datta ka na.

Now, what time was it that I was going to meet Tanaka?

3. Indicates a hope or muted request: "I wonder."

この仕事、頼んでいい**かな**。

Kono shigoto, tanonde ii ka na.

I wonder if I could ask [you to do] this job. / Can I ask you to take care of this work?

明日の朝早く会社に来てもらえる**かな**。

Ashita no asa hayaku kaisha ni kite moraeru ka na.

I wonder if you could come to the office early tomorrow morning. / Could you come to the office early tomorrow morning?

58 — KASHIRA | かしら

Note: The usages of *kashira* are essentially the same as those of *ka na*, except that they are mostly employed by women.

1. Indicates uncertainty: "I wonder."

社長さん、今日何時に会社へいらっしゃいます**かしら**。

*Shachō-san, kyō nanji ni kaisha e irasshaimasu **kashira**.*

I wonder what time the president will come to the office today.

この機械の使い方、ご存じでいらっしゃいます**かしら**。

*Kono kikai no tsukaikata, gozonji de irasshaimasu **kashira**.*

I wonder if you're acquainted with how this machine is run.

2. Indicates a question to oneself: "I wonder."

もう帰ってもいいの**かしら**。

Mō kaette mo ii no kashira.

I wonder if it's all right to leave now [if I can leave now].

こんなすてきなプレゼントをもらって、いいの**かし
ら**。

Konna suteki na purezento o moratte, ii no kashira.

I wonder if I should accept such a lovely present. / Oh, you shouldn't have. / Oh, what a lovely present! I don't deserve it.

3. Indicates a hope or muted request: "I wonder."

今晩私の宿題を手伝ってくれる**かしら**。

Konban watashi no shukudai o tetsudatte kureru kashira.

I wonder if you would help me with my homework tonight. / Do you think you could help me with my homework tonight?

コンピューターの使い方、教えていただける**かしら**。

Konpyūtā no tsukaikata, oshiete itadakeru kashira.

I wonder if you could teach me how to operate the computer. / Could you possibly teach me how to operate the computer?

59 — | NA | な

1. Indicates emotion. Mostly used by men.

Note: *Na* in this usage is often lengthened to *nā*.

あの人はすばらしい**なあ**。

Ano hito wa subarashii nā.

She's really great [something]!

きれいな星だ**なあ**。

Kirei na hoshi da nā.

What a beautiful star!

2. Asks for another person's agreement. Used by men.

あの車は新車だよな。

Ano kuruma wa shinsha da yo na.

That's a new car, right? / That's a new car, I bet.

あそこは寒いな。

Asoko wa samui na.

It's cold there, isn't it.

3. Softens the effect of an assertion.

あの人はなかなか立派な人だと思うな。

Ano hito wa nakanaka rippa na hito da to omou na.

I really think [I'd say] that he is a fine, upstanding person.

この映画はよくなかったな。

Kono eiga wa yoku nakatta na.

This movie just wasn't very good.

4. Softens a command or request (first example, a woman speaking with typical *kudasai na* pattern; second example, a man).

成田まで行って下さいな。

Narita made itte kudasai na.

Narita [Airport], please [if you please].

明日必ず来いな。

Ashita kanarazu koi na.

Be sure to come tomorrow.

5. Indicates a prohibition. Used by men.

絶対にあいつに会うな。

Zettai ni aitsu ni au na.

Stay away from that bum, you hear. / Keep clear of that guy.

もうあのバーに行くな。

Mō ano bā ni iku na.

Don't go to that bar ever again! / No more going to that bar, hear.

60 — SA | さ

1. Softens an assertion. Used mostly by men.

明日の高橋さんのパーティーには、もちろん行くさ。

Ashita no Takahashi-san no pātī ni wa, mochiron iku sa.

I'm going to Takahashi's party tomorrow, of course.

それより、こっちのセーターの方が大きいさ。

Sore yori, kotchi no sētā no hō ga ōkii sa.

This sweater's bigger than that one, I'd say.

2. Indicates a critical response to something.

あんな無能な社員を入れるから、会社が伸びないのさ。

Anna munō na shain o ireru kara, kaisha ga nobinai no sa.

It's because they hire incompetent people like him that the company doesn't grow.

あの人のやりそうなことさ。

Ano hito no yarisō na koto sa.

It's something he would do. / It's just like him.

61 — KOTO | こと

Note: *Koto*, as a sentence-ending particle, is used mainly by women.

1. Indicates emotion.

この花の色の美しいこと。

Kono hana no iro no utsukushii koto.

What an exquisite color this flower has!

おいしいお料理ですこと。

Oishii oryōri desu koto.

What marvelously delicious food!

2. Indicates a suggestion or invitation.

どこかへお花見に行きませんこと。

Doko ka e ohanami ni ikimasen koto.

Shall we go flower-viewing somewhere?

一度クイーンエリザベス号に乗ってみませんこと。

Ichido Kuīnerizabesu-gō ni notte mimasen koto.

Shall we just once go aboard the *Queen Elizabeth*?

62 — -KKE | っけ

Note: *-Kke* follows V-*ta* and Adj-*ta* forms. In feminine speech, the verb forms tend to be *desu*, *deshita*, and V-*mashita*.

1. Indicates a muted question in cases when there is information shared with an interlocutor that the speaker is trying to recall.

明日の結婚式は、何時に始まるんでしたっけ。

Ashita no kekkon-shiki wa, nanji ni hajimaru-n deshita-kke.

What time was the wedding going to start tomorrow? / The wedding tomorrow–what time was it going to start?

あなたの家はどこだったっけ。

Anata no ie wa doko datta-kke.

Now, where was your house? / Where did you say your house was?

2. Indicates that the speaker is remembering something from the distant past.

この辺に学校があったっけ。

Kono hen ni gakkō ga atta-kke.

Didn't there used to be a school around here? / I seem to remember that there was a school around here.

あの人とよく酒を飲んだっけ。

Ano hito to yoku sake o nonda-kke.

Back in the old days I used to go drinking a lot with him. / I remember going drinking with him quite a bit.

63 — | -TTEBA | ってば

1. Indicates annoyance with another person.

明日までにできなければ困るってば。

Ashita made ni dekinakereba komaru-tteba.

I'm telling you, there's going to be trouble if it's not done by tomorrow.

来年では遅すぎるってば。

Rainen de wa ososugiru-tteba.

Next year will be too late, I'm telling you.

2. Indicates an indirect command or prohibition.

そんなことをしたら、だめだってば。

Sonna koto o shitara, dame da-tteba.

I'm telling you that it's no good if you do such a thing. / I wouldn't do that if I were you.

コンピューターを使わなければ、できないってば。

Konpyūtā o tsukawanakereba, dekinai-tteba.

I'm telling you that you can't do it unless you use the computer. / You won't get anywhere unless you use the computer, I'd say.

64 — | -I | い

1. Following *da* or *ka*, indicates an informal question. Used mostly by men.

どうして新宿まで行ったんだい。

Dō shite Shinjuku made itta-n dai.

Why'd you go as far as [all the way to] Shinjuku?

昨日どこで飲んだんだい。

Kinō doko de nonda-n dai.

Where'd you go drinking yesterday?

またアメリカに出張かい、大変だな。

Mata Amerika ni shutchō kai, taihen da na.

Off to the U.S. on business again? Hang in there.

あの人、元気だったかい。

Ano hito, genki datta kai.

How was she? / How's she getting along?

65 — MONO | もの

Note: The primary meaning of *mono* as a sentence-ending particle is "because" or "the reason is," and in the individual usages below, with their special connotations, this meaning is still vaguely felt.

1. Indicates an excuse, a dissatisfaction, or a desire to be indulged or pampered. Used by women.

a) Reason or excuse.

あの映画は面白くないんです**もの**。だから、行かなかったのよ。

*Ano eiga wa omoshiroku nai-n desu **mono**. Da kara, ikanakatta no yo.*

That movie is simply too boring. That's why I didn't go.

どうして食べないんだい。
この料理、嫌いなんです**もの**。

Dō shite tabenai-n dai.
*Kono ryōri, kirai nan desu **mono**.*

Why aren't you eating?
I simply don't like this food.

b) Dissatisfaction (with a woman speaking).

課長の仕事はやりたくないわ。下の者に冷たいんです**もの**。

*Kachō no shigoto wa yaritaku nai wa. Shita no mono ni tsumetai-n desu **mono**.*

I don't want to work for the section chief. He's so cold to those working under him.

竹内さんとは一緒に仕事をしたくないのよ。ちっとも働かないんだもの。

*Takeuchi-san to wa issho ni shigoto o shitaku nai no yo. Chitto mo hatarakanai-n da **mono**.*

I don't want to work with Takeuchi. He just doesn't do anything [doesn't work].

c) Desire to be indulged or pampered.

出かけましょうよ。たまには外で食事がしたいんですもの。

*Dekakemashō yo. Tama ni wa soto de shokuji ga shitai-n desu **mono**.*

Come on, let's go out. I'd like to eat out once in a while.

あれ欲しいですもの。買ってもいいでしょう。

*Are hoshii desu **mono**. Katte mo ii deshō.*

I want it [so badly]. It's all right if I buy it, isn't it?

66 — | ZE | ぜ |

Note: Adds force to a sentence. When it overlaps with *zo* (#67), it is somewhat less emphatic. *Ze* is used mostly by men.

1. Used to make a declaration to someone or underscore a point.

先に行くぜ。

*Saki ni iku **ze**.*

I'm going on ahead. / Leaving now. See you there.

その仕事、君に頼んだぜ。

*Sono shigoto, kimi ni tanonda **ze**.*

I'm counting on you to do that job. / It's [the job's] up to you now.

頑張るぜ。

Ganbaru ze.

I'm going to give it my best shot. / I'm hanging tough.

67 — ZO | ぞ

Note: *Zo* adds force to a sentence in a more emphatic manner than *ze* (#66). Used mostly by men.

1. Indicates a command or threat.

そろそろ会議を始めるぞ。

Sorosoro kaigi o hajimeru zo.

Let's get the meeting under way.

今度そんなことをしたら、絶対に許さないぞ。

Kondo sonna koto o shitara, zettai ni yurusanai zo.

If you do that again, I'm not going to let you get away with it. / If you do anything like that again, you're going to pay for it.

その仕事、君に頼んだぞ。

Sono shigoto, kimi ni tanonda zo.

I'm expecting you to get the job done. / You'd better get cracking on that job.

2. Adds force to words of self-encouragement or self-urging.

頑張るぞ。

Ganbaru zo.

I can do it! / Make way. Here I come.

今度こそ成功するぞ。

Kondo koso seikō suru zo.

I'm going to make it this time. / This time I'm coming up a winner.

68 — | MONO KA | ものか |

Note: Men tend to use the forms *mono ka* and *mon ka*; women *mono desu ka* and *mon desu ka*.

1. Emphasizes a determination not to do something by means of a rhetorical question.

あんな所、もう行く**もんか**。

*Anna tokoro, mō iku **mon ka**.*

I wouldn't be caught dead going there again.

あんな人と一緒に仕事ができる**もんですか**。

*Anna hito to issho ni shigoto ga dekiru **mon desu ka**.*

I wouldn't work with her again if my life depended on it.

69 — | NI | に |

Note: *Ni* commonly follows *darō*, *deshō*, and V-*tarō*, and essentially has the same meaning as *no ni* (#30, no. 2), although the latter is more common.

1. Expresses regret that something is over and can't be regained: "despite the fact that, if only."

ほかの人がやったら、もっと早くできたでしょう**に**。

*Hoka no hito ga yattara, motto hayaku dekita deshō **ni**.*

Despite the fact that it could have been finished much sooner if someone else had done it, [unfortunately that was not the case]. / It could have been finished much sooner if only someone else had done it.

もう少し待っていたら、雨がやんだろう**に**。

*Mō sukoshi matte itara, ame ga yandarō **ni**.*

Despite the fact that if we had waited a little longer, the rain might have stopped [we didn't wait]. / If only we had waited a little longer, the rain might have let up.

Index

Numbers in bold indicate main entries.

adjectives of ability, 19
adjectives of desire, 18
adjectives of emotion, 18–19
adjectives of necessity, 18
ai suru, 55

-ba, **83–85**, 108
bakari, **67–69**, 72, 73
bakari ni, 69
bakashi, 67
bakkari, 67
bakkashi, 67

dai. See *-i*.
dai nari shō nari, 102
dake, **69–72**, 73, 74
dake atte, 70–71
dake ni, 70–71
dake no koto wa aru, 70
dano, 98, **99–100**
darō ni, 124
datte, 27
de, **42–45**
de mo, **27–29**, 108
-de mo (*-te mo*), **26–27**
de wa, 12
-de wa (*-te wa*), 12, **102–3**
-de wa ikenai, 103
-de wa komaru, 103
-de wa naranai, 103
dekireba, 84
dekiru, 17
deshō ni, 124
dokoro, **104**
dokoro ka, 104

e, **52**

ga, 10–11, **12–23**, 76, 79, 81
gurai (*kurai*), **64–65**

hayai ka (V + *ga hayai ka*), 23
heta na, 19
hitsuyō da, 18
hodo, **65–67**
hoshii, 18

-i, **120–21**
ieba, 84
ienai (*tomo . . . tomo ienai*), 97
iru, 18
iu, 31

jōzu na, 19

ka, **39–42**, 100
ka na, **114–15**
kai. See *-i*.
kanashii, 19
kara, **52–56**, 63, 75, 76, 106
kashira, 114, **115–16**
-ke. See *-kke*.
kedo, 76
keredo, 76
keredomo, **76–78**, 79, 81
kikoeru, 17, 60
kirai da, 19
kiri, 72, **74–75**
kiku, 31, 55
kiyō na, 19

-kke, **119–20**
kochira koso, 110
koso, **109–10**
koto, **118–19**
kowai, 19
kurai (gurai), **64–65**
kuse ni, **80–81**

made, **56–58**
made mo nai, 57–58
meirei suru, 55
mieru, 17, 60
mo, **23–25**
mon ka, 124
mono, **121–22**
mono de, 76
mono ka, 124
mono nara, **88–89**
mono no, **81–82**
mono o, 91

na, **116–17**
nā, 116
nado, **37–39**
-nagara, **91–92**
nan nari, 101
nanka, 37
nanzo, 37
nara, **87–88**
nari, **100–102**
naru, 30
nazo, 37
ne, **110–11**, 112
nē, 110
ni, **45–51**, 52, 54, **124**
ni motozuku, 51
ni natte iru, 49
ni shite wa, 102
ni wa, 12
ni yoru, 51
no, 16, **58–61**

no de, 55, **75–76**
nomi, 72, **73–74**
nomi narazu, 73–74
no ni, **79–80**, 81, 124

o, 12, **61–64**
omou, 31
onomatopoeia, 32

potential form of verbs, 17

sa, **118**
sae, **108–9**
shi, **94–95**
shika, **72–73**, 74
shikaru, 55
shinpai suru, 19
shiraberu, 55
sugu, 32
suki da, 19
sura, **109**
suru, 12, 17, 62

-tagaru form of verbs, 62
-tai form of verbs, 18, 62
-tara, **85–87**, 108
-tari, **92–94**
-tarō ni, 124
-te mo (-de mo), **26–27**
-te wa (-de wa), 12, **102–3**
-te wa ikenai, 103
-te wa komaru, 103
-te wa naranai, 103
-teba. See *-tteba*.
to, **29–34**, 35
to ii ga, 22
to iu yori, 106
to ka, **36–37**, 98, 99
to shite wa, 102. See also *toshite*.
to wa, **34–35**

tokoro, 68, **89–91**
tokoro de, **78–79**
tokoro ga, **82–83**
tokui na, 19
tomo, **95–97**
tomo arō N + *ga*, 96
toshite, **104–5**. See also *to shite wa*.
-ttara, 86
-tteba, **120**

ureshii, 19

verbs of emotion, 18–19
verbs of necessity, 18
verbs of perception, 60
verbs of sensation, 17

wa, **10–12**
wa (contrasted with *ga*), 13, 14, 15, 17, 18, 19, 20
wa (sentence-ending), **113**
wa yo, 113
wakaru, 17

ya, **35–36**, 98
ya ina ya, 36
yara, **97–99**
yo, **112–13**
yori, **105–8**
yori hoka nai, 107
yori ka, 105
yori mo, 105

ze, **122–23**
zo, 122, **123**